EDWIN'S LETTERS

BY THE SAME AUTHOR

NAVAL HISTORY
With Ensigns Flying
Submarine Victory
Battle of the Java Sea
Crete 1941: the Battle at Sea
Japan's War at Sea: Pearl Harbor to the Coral Sea
Royal Admirals
A Companion to the Royal Navy
The Illustrated Armada Handbook
The Atlantic Star 1939–45
Christopher Columbus: Master of the Atlantic
Queen Mary and the Cruiser: The Curacoa Disaster (with Patrick Holmes)
Battles and Honours of the Royal Navy
Malta Convoys 1940–42

SOCIAL HISTORY
The Canning Story 1785–1985
Churchill: The Member for Woodford

BIBLIOGRAPHY
Compton Mackenzie: a Bibliography (with Joyce Thomas)

JUVENILE
How Ships are Made

Edwin's Letters

A Fragment of Life
1940–43

Edited by David A. Thomas

CASSELL&CO
A WINDRUSH PRESS BOOK

Cassell & Co
Wellington House, 125 Strand
London WC2R 0BB

in association with
The Windrush Press
Windrush House, Adlestrop, Moreton-in-Marsh
Gloucestershire GL56 0YN

British Library Cataloguing-in-Publication Data

A catalogue record for this book is available from the British Library

ISBN 0-304-36161-5

Designed by Yvonne Dedman
Printed and bound in Great Britain by
MPG Books Ltd, Bodmin, Cornwall

CONTENTS

Last night more than 600 aircraft of Bomber Command, in the biggest night operation this year, heavily attacked two of the most important centres of German armament production.

Lancasters and Halifaxes in great force penetrated to the Skoda armament works at Pilsen in Czechoslovakia. Thirty-seven machines are missing.

At the same time, another force of Wellingtons, Stirlings and Halifaxes attacked the armament centre of Mannheim-Ludwigshaven. Here, eighteen are missing.

Preliminary reports indicate that both attacks were concentrated and successful.

Air Ministry communiqué
17 April 1943

PREFACE

Edwin was born in São Paulo on 23 July 1921. He was the first-born son of Helen and Edwin Gordon Thomas senior, an official of the Bank of London and South America who enjoyed overseas tours of duty to the Brazilian cities of São Paulo and Pernambuco.

Four years after Edwin's birth another son, David, was born in England, and some years later still an only daughter, Margaret, completed the family. Peggy, or Pegs, as she was called by the family, was a 'Paulista', that is born in São Paulo, like her elder brother.

Edwin was killed at the age of twenty-one with six other young airmen who formed the crew of a Halifax bomber, K for Kathleen, of No. 78 Squadron, Royal Air Force. His body, with those of his comrades, lies in the tranquillity and serenity of a war cemetery in the battle-scarred Somme, tended with devoted care in the park-like beauty created by the British War Graves Commission.

Edwin's early ambition was to be a pilot in the Fleet Air Arm, but he never attained it. Equally elusive was a Royal Air Force pilot's brevet. Neither a naval nor an air force commission was within his reach. Disappointment followed disappointment as he failed successive examinations until he resigned himself to achieving nothing greater than membership of a bomber's aircrew. Most of his service life was directed to this end and he attained the rank of Sergeant Wireless Operator/Air Gunner. But in the end neither rank nor brevet mattered. Death for Edwin and his friends was a common denominator.

His letters to his mother during this period of service have been preserved with meticulous care. With a maternal prescience, as if aware of ultimate tragedy, she kept the whole collection swathed in ribbons until her dying day twenty-seven years after her son's death. The letters span a period of nearly two and a half years, a fragment of autobiography that averaged a letter every ten days while Edwin was away from home: a creditable filial performance.

This collection of Edwin's letters, together with supporting documents, other items of official correspondence and sundry letters arising from the loss of the Halifax aircrew, are reproduced in this book as they were written or typed, including occasional errors of spelling, grammar and punctuation. They tell their own story. They cannot be judged by any literary standard because they relate quite simply the trivia of a young man's thoughts and feelings during wartime service. Cigarettes were more important than culture; sweets, rations, clothing coupons, pay-day and postal-order allowances also loomed large at the time. The cinema and popular wireless music were more fulfilling than enduring musical compositions and literature. Such ephemeral pleasures were sought because life itself was transitory. Friends and comrades – barely out of their teens – were with you one day and in a prisoner-of-war camp the next ... if they were lucky.

The letters, however, tell a story, much more than just the activities of a young airman training for war. They unfold a tale of anguish by bereavement. After the loss of the Halifax bomber each succeeding letter, whether of kindly condolence or official communication, seemed to probe the wound ever more sharply, adding to rather than easing the pain. Yet this story is but a tiny part of the great grief of The Second World War that pervaded the continents of the world and which can never be quantified. It is easy to count the losses, but impossible to compute the pain.

Edwin's service in the RAF was undistinguished – except by his sacrifice of life – and his death was merely one among tens of millions who died tragically between 1939 and 1945. His story begins in documentary form in the year 1936 and now sixty-eight years later this chronicle of his life, cut short by war, is a further memorial.

David A. Thomas

PART ONE

GROWING UP

1936–40

BOROUGH OF LEYTON
EDUCATION COMMITTEE

Testimonial as to the character of Edwin G. Thomas,
Pupil at Canterbury Road Senior School.

25th March 1936

Edwin G. Thomas has been a pupil at the above school since May 1935 and has passed through the Third Year Group. He has been regular and punctual in his attendance, he is a thoroughly honest and trust-worthy lad, and his conduct has been excellent.

He has shown earnestness and painstaking ability in his work, in manner he is quiet, serious and gentlemanly, and he is of good intelligence.

He should make a most reliable worker.

T. H. Moore Head Teacher

Will employers kindly return this testimonial to applicant. THE JUVENILE EMPLOYMENT BUREAU, Kirkdale Road School, Leytonstone, is always available for advice and assistance in obtaining suitable employment.

A.M. Form 180

In any subsequent communication
respecting this letter, please quote
Air Ministry reference: S 7e/552

The Under-Secretary of State for Air has to acknowledge your letter of 1/5/39 and Birth Certificate, which will receive attention.

Air Ministry, Kingsway, London WC2   5/5/39

Snaresbrook College
Woodford Road E18

19th July 1940

<u>To Whom It May Concern</u>

Since leaving school Mr E. Thomas has been a student at this college and has received special coaching in arithmetic, mathematics (including trigonometry), Mechanics and Physics. He has certainly reached secondary school standard.

Mr Thomas readily grasps any instructions given and his method of execution is particularly careful and accurate.

He would, I am sure, work conscientiously and perform with exactitude any task entrusted to him.

(Signed) M.W. Hanger (Principal)

Any replies should be addressed to: HMS St Vincent
The Commanding Officer   Gosport
                                                            Hants

                                                            18 – 9 – 40

NAME: E. G. Thomas Esq.
ADDRESS: 38 Highstone Avenue
          Wanstead
          Essex

With reference to your application for training as Pilot or Observer in the Naval Air Branch, you are required to report to HMS St Vincent at 0900 on Tuesday 1st October 1940 for an interview by the Selection Committee and Medical Examination by the Central Air Medical Board, as to your fitness to fly.

A railway warrant is attached, which should be exchanged for a ticket at the Railway Booking Office.

Arrangements can be made for your accommodation in St Vincent for the preceding night, should you so desire. The accommodation, however, cannot be guaranteed after 6pm and the last meal at St Vincent is given at 6.30pm.

                                           Lieut. Cdr.
                                           Air Branch Training Officer

A. M. Pamphlet 96
2nd Edition

ROYAL AIR FORCE VOLUNTEER RESERVE
RECRUITS VOLUNTEERING IN EMERGENCY FOR SERVICE AS MEMBERS OF AIRCRAFT CREWS

Introductory

Enlistment is offered to men of good education who volunteer for service in aircraft crews. Aircraft crews consist of pilots, observers, wireless operators (aircrew) and air gunners. Airmen of all these classes will be drawn from recruits who enlist in the first instance for training as "aircraft crew". Applicants must pass a special medical examination and must be adjudged as suitable by a selection panel. The limits of age are:

Airman Pilot	
Air Observer	18–20
Wireless Operator (aircrew)	
Air Gunner	

  An applicant for enlistment may specify whether he is desirous of being trained as a pilot or observer should he prove suitable, or in one of the other trades mentioned above. Those who prove unsuitable for crew duties will be given the alternatives of (a) re-mustering to aircrafthand general duties (b) re-mustering to another trade for which they are suitable, or (c) taking their discharge.

2. General Conditions

(i)   Applicants must be up to the School Certificate or an equivalent standard in education.
(ii) Men in receipt of a disability pension are ineligible for enlistment.
(iii) Men must be willing to be vaccinated or re-vaccinated.
(iv) The period of service in all cases will be for the duration of the present Emergency.
(v)   On acceptance the recruit will be required to complete the Attestation Form (Form 2167) and be attested in the RAFVR.

3. Pay During Training

Recruits selected as suitable for training as pilots, observers or air gunners will undergo an initial course of ground training during which they will be mustered as aircrafthands, Group V, under training aircraft crew and classified Aircraftman 2nd Class, receiving pay at the rate of 2s od per day. An airman who proceeds for training as a pilot will be re-mustered to Group II, and re-classified as Leading Aircraftman, and will receive pay at the rate of 5s od a day, plus flying instructional pay at 2s od a day while under-going training. An airman who proceeds to training as an observer will be re-mustered to Group II and re-classified as Leading Aircraftman and will receive pay at the rate of 5s od a day, plus flying instructional pay of 1s 6d a day while undergoing training. Those entered for training as wireless operator (aircrew) or proceeding for training as air gunner will be re-mustered as aircrafthands, Group V under training wireless operator (aircrew) or air gunner, and will retain the classification of Aircraftman, 2nd Class, receiving pay at the rate of 2s od per day [...]

4. [...] A limited number of airman pilots and observers will be selected, on the results attained on passing out of training, for appointment to commissioned rank ...

5. [...] Airmen also receive free accommodation, food and clothing (or money allowances instead) and medical attention.

N.B. This leaflet contains a brief outline only and it must be understood that its provisions are subject in all respects to the detailed regulations which have been issued, or may from time to time be issued, by the Air Council: in particular nothing in this summary may be used to support a claim to any rate of pay etc.

AIR MINISTRY

Reference: CRC/CU/E

<u>All communications should be addressed to the Officer-in-Charge</u>

From: Officer-in-Charge
        Royal Air Force Section
        Combined Recruiting Centre, ROMFORD

To: Mr E. G. Thomas   Date: 23 Oct 1940

THIS LETTER SHOULD BE SHOWN ON ARRIVAL AT THE RECRUITING CENTRE

Sir,

With reference to your application for enlistment into the Royal Air Force Volunteer Reserve, it is requested that you will report at this centre on 29 Oct 1940 at 9.15am.

2. The vacancy for which you are being considered is that of Aircrew.

3. You will be required to proceed to a Receiving Centre for Attestation.

4. You may not, however, be required for immediate service, and on attestation you may be returned to civilian life pending recall to the Service, during which time no pay or emoluments will be issued.

5. It is suggested, therefore, that if you are in employment, you obtain two or three days leave in order to proceed to the Receiving Centre, so that if you are not required for immediate service you may, after attestation, continue with your civilian employment, pending your recall for service. The Attestation Officer will advise you as to the probable period of any deferment of service, and before being recalled you will be given approximately ten days notice.

6. If you are required for immediate service you will be permitted, if necessary, to return home for a limited period to settle your business and private affairs.

7. [...] You should bring with you the following:

(a) Your Ration Card.

(b) Your shaving kit etc and sufficient clothing for two or three days. You are recommended to bring an overcoat or waterproof.

(c) Your National Health and Insurance Cards, or, if not available, their numbers.

(d) Your civilian gas mask.

(e) Your Registration Card (if registered under the National Service (Armed Forces) Act).

(f) (If married) Your marriage certificate and birth certificates of children, if possible.

> I am, Sir,
> Your Obedient Servant,
>   A. EMERSON
> for Officer-in-Charge
> Royal Air Force Section
> Combined Recruiting Centre

Part Two

IN THE RAF

1940–43

Babbacombe Hotel
Babbacombe Down
Torquay
Devon

5th November 1940

My dear Mother,

I arrived here safely last night – but late because of a railway smash further up the line. Babbacombe is pleasant enough although the hotel is a little distance from our mess rooms, so at meal times we walk out with our knives and forks like the soldiers billeted in Cambridge Park [Wanstead].

We haven't been issued with our uniforms or kit yet nor have we had an air raid warning since we have been here. I hope it wasn't too bad at home last night.

I expect to be here a fortnight during which time we drill and learn the fundamentals of fractions and decimals before going on to Initial Training Wing. There, if we pass, we get promoted to Leading Aircraftman. In all, the ITW course should last eight weeks.

Yours affectionately
Edwin

P.S. I haven't had time to buy a watch yet.
Also do not know about sending money home
because have not received any yet and get paid
fortnightly (I think).

Babbacombe Hotel
Babbacombe Down
Torquay
Devon

9th November 1940

My dear Mother,

Thank you for the parcel, which I received today.

I still haven't bought the watch for myself ... We poor blighters who came in on Monday will not get any pay until <u>next</u> Friday – and then only ten bob! I have had to spend ten shillings of the thirty bob I had ... having to buy such things as cleaning equipment, towel, soap, toothbrush, mirror and so on.

I've hardly been smoking because of a cold – so the money has not been wasted. And I thought you'd like a letter with the RAF crest on it – so I bought some writing paper for 1/9d.

We were supplied with our kit today – except for the cap badges. The uniform fits me perfectly although some fellows look quite laughable in theirs.

I pass the time nicely in the evenings at the YMCA reading room, which has a canteen upstairs.

The food is delicious and I am very happy. We start training next week in earnest: so far we have only completed one day's work – which was regimental drill. We have still not had an air raid warning.

Your affectionate
Edwin 1270671

P. S. When having finished course at ITW ... if pass
as pilot or observer one gets Leading Aircraftman
badge and 5/6d per day.

The Battle of Britain had been fought out under the blue skies and hot sunshine of the summer. 'The Few', as Prime Minister Winston Churchill named the young pilots in their Spitfire and Hurricane fighters, fought bitter daytime battles and the imminent invasion of England was set aside.

London had borne the brunt of the battle but worse was to follow. The Blitz was unleashed upon the nation and practically all major cities were seriously damaged, and hundreds of people were killed.

The Thomas family, like most of the population, sheltered from the bombing at night and endured the discomfort of five sleeping in a concrete shelter at the bottom of their garden in Wanstead, on the outskirts of London's east end. Father worked by day at the Town Hall; Edwin made preparations to enlist in the RAF. The two younger children attended high school and mother bonded the whole into a family. The night-time Blitz continued unabated for months. An incendiary bomb crashed through the roof of their home but managed to avoid igniting the house.

Babbacombe Hotel
Babbacombe Down
Torquay
Devon

13th November 1940

My dear Mother,

We have been told that we will be posted on Friday evening or Saturday morning, so after you receive this letter it would be better if you didn't write until you hear from me. We have heard that it might be Aberystwyth (if that's how you spell it). Babbacombe has been pleasant enough – close by the sea but away from the crowds of Torquay.

I shall be sending my suitcase home this week with my old clothes. We are going to be paid on Friday – but only 10/–d. It is amazing how money is spent on necessities such as copying ink, the VR badges that aren't on the uniform and cost 6d a pair: you need a pair each for the great coat and the tunic – plus the 'eagle' shoulder badges.

I shall be going to an ITW this week where I hope to pass the general course to become an LAC (Leading Aircraftman). Nearly all pass this.

Then on to an EFTS (Elementary Flying Training School). This is where 50–75% pilots pip. But we all stand a goodish chance.

I so hope you are not having too many air raids. I always look in the <u>Telegraph</u> and read about the evening's happenings and see that you have had one or two early All Clears. We have not had an Alert since we have been here.

Dear Mother, when addressing letters to me always put my number after the name and A/C in front please.

We haven't been wearing our uniforms because of the missing cap badges – but have been allowed to wear RAF shirt, collars, tie and boots. And don't the boots keep us busy!

You polish for hours to get a feeble shine!

Now, as regards money matters: I have about ten bob, plus your five shillings, which was very kind of you. I think the best thing to do about my pay is to put 10/–d away fortnightly, leaving 15/–d – that is 7/6d pocket money for each week, which will be fine.

Regarding food: for breakfast yesterday we had porridge, fried egg and mashed potatoes, bread and butter, marmalade and a terrific mug or two of tea. For dinner: a lovely stew with potatoes and veg: for sweet: an apple conglomeration with custard – and an apple. For tea: plenty of liver and gravy, bread and butter, jam and a piece of fruitcake. Cake everyday. Supper: jug of milk, liver between two crusts and a slice of cake.

We get up at 6.30 and walk a quarter of a mile to breakfast. It is always better to be early for meals because the early food is hotter.

Love and kisses
Edwin

P.S. Thursday morning: it appears that I am not
      going to Wales this weekend but to Cambridge
      next week – which is much nearer London, of course.
      I am really one of the lucky ones because out of our
      Flight of 50 about 30 are going to Newquay and the
      rest to Cambridge. So if I get only a few days leave
      I can get home easily.

Babbacombe Hotel
Babbacombe Down
Torquay
Devon

21st November 1940

My Dear Mother,

It was quite a shock this morning to receive the registered letter and also a surprise to hear you hadn't received a letter from me for so long. I expect you will have received my letter posted a week ago today and also the seven page letter enclosed with the suitcase I sent home last Saturday ... As a precaution I am going to have this letter registered and expressed so that you receive it tomorrow.

'On parade, Flight 3!'

The different Flights have just been told where they will be posted. Four fellows in our Flight have been left behind again. All four – including myself – have slight eye defects. But we hope to get to Cambridge next week.

I have completely recovered from my last two inoculations and vaccinations although I don't think the latter have 'taken'. Yesterday we had yet another.

Thank you for buying a lighter for Christmas. I can't think of anything else I'd like.

I am very fit and happy and am having some good times.

I haven't been to the cinema because the films are frightfully old: for example, Beau Geste and Good-bye Mr Chips. But I have been to some good concerts, which only cost nine pence a time. In the evenings I invariably go out with the fellows to play billiards, snooker or table tennis and end up with a glass of Devonshire cider.

Last Saturday I received my first pay of £1.

By the way, Ken Farnes is here in No. 2 Flight. He has got to wait three months for a uniform because the RAF can't find one to fit him.* All the fellows in our Flight are either University or public school men. One I had supper with last week was an old rowing blue and a charming fellow.

---

* The England and Essex fast bowler was very tall. He was killed later when the aircraft he piloted was shot down.

I am going to a concert tonight with the boys. We are too broke to get tipsy. One of the fellows is playing the piano at the concert. He plays very well and can syncopate, too.

Love to all,
Edwin

No. 2 Flight
A Squadron
No. 2 ITW
Pembroke College
Cambridge

16/12/40 7 o'clock

My dear Mother,

As you can see by my address I am now at Cambridge, supposedly the best ITW in England. I arrived last Saturday at nine o'clock.

This morning we attended three lectures – maths, anti-gas and signalling in morse. This afternoon I was interviewed by a Pilot Officer. It seems that I didn't come out too well in the grading tests at Babbacombe. 'Don't worry,' he said, 'the grading test is more difficult than the maths exam.' In this test one has to get 60% or more. If you are 'out' you have a chance of re-mustering as a Wireless/Operator/Air Gunner. I am going to have special maths swotting with friends after hours.

At this ITW we get up at 6, have breakfast at 7, dinner at 12.30 and high tea at 5.45. The food is absolutely wonderful. We have our meals in the dining hall of Pembroke. The tables are highly polished and run the whole length of the hall.

I was paid 30/–d last Friday and enclose a postal order for 6/6d.

It is comforting to be less than 60 miles from home and I am looking forward to some leave at the end of this course, which will last about ten weeks. I am still with my friends and share a bedroom with Roley and Mickey. We are also provided with a living room furnished with a settee, three armchairs, a writing desk, two other chairs and – wonder of wonders – a fire! These stone colleges are very cold.

Last Sunday Malcolm, Mickey, Roley, Gerry and I went to Trinity College and visited the marvellous chapel. Tonight we are going to Frank's room to have an hour's work on morse as he is lucky enough to have a morse tapper.

What, Mother dear, had I better do about Christmas presents? Will you please reply as soon as possible. I should like to know that you are all safe and happy.

Yours affectionately,
Edwin

No. 2 Flight
A Squadron
No. 2 ITW
Pembroke College
Cambridge

21st December 1940

My dear Mother,

None of us has any time to spare here. We start work at 0800 hours and finish at 1700 and haven't any time to shop or buy Christmas cards. I'm sorry I shan't be able to send any RAF-crested cards because they are absolutely unobtainable in Cambridge.

I was paid a pound yesterday. We just happened to arrive in pay week. So I enclose a 5/–d postal order and hope this will be sufficient for you. I am sure to have to spend a spot of money with my friends over Christmas.

I put my name down for boxing last Thursday and in the afternoon had three rounds with a fellow of my weight. But the poor fellow had never boxed before and his defence was an opponent's dream. Later, the Corporal Instructor (Harry Mizler, the boxer) bounced medicine balls on our stomachs to strengthen the muscles. Did it make us gasp! Then we went for a two-mile run round the park.

After tea that evening I swotted arithmetic with Gerry and Mickey until nearly ten. If you want to be a pilot you have to work like blazes.

I have just finished today – Saturday – at 4.15. But _if_ I get through the maths test it will all have been worthwhile. I must say that the maths exam is worrying me: but I shall do my best.

Incidentally, Pembroke is one of the many colleges, which have been taken over – Jesus, St John's, Magdalene, Christ's. They are marvellous.

Lots of love for a very happy Christmas.

Affectionately

Edwin

No. 2 Flight
A Squadron
No. 2 ITW
Pembroke College
Cambridge

Christmas evening 1940

My dear Mother,

I opened the parcel this morning. I think the cigarette lighter and the tobacco pouch are very good. Thank you, Dad, and please thank Peggy for the book and David for the diary. I am very pleased with everything.

At this ITW everyone has to do a spot of guard duty and sleep in the guardroom all night. I and three others were chosen for duty tonight.

We had a jolly good Christmas dinner – no turkey – but pork, baked potatoes, then Christmas pudding, with a pint of beer each. Gerry is TT so I drank his. We then went out and celebrated with a drink of cider.

Incidentally, we attended a lecture this morning and even did PT for an hour in the open air as usual.

I have seen the pay accounts fellow and have made an allotment so that you will be able to draw from the post office 7/–d each week. This will take effect from January 9th. I hope this will be sufficient. I will be paid full pay here at the rate of 35/–d a fortnight.

Visited the RAF club last night for a social and dance. I was rather dubious about my chances with a partner; when I told her I had never danced before she said 'I am surprised,' but I really think she meant 'I am not surprised!'

Going to tea tomorrow with Malcolm, Mickey and Roley. Malcolm was invited by a lady at the YMCA last Friday, and she asked him to bring along three friends. People do a lot of this charitable work in Cambridge.

It is Sunday now. I am sorry I haven't posted the letter. Malcolm, Mickey, Roley and I had a marvellous time at the Boxing Day tea party – and Malcolm and I have been invited to tea this afternoon. The family consists of Mr and Mrs Rudd, son and four daughters. Oh Boy!

Yours affectionately
Edwin

No. 2 Flight
No. 2 ITW
Pembroke College
Cambridge

2nd January 1941

My dear Mother,

Will you please wish Peggy many happy returns of the day (for the 3rd). I have been wanting to buy her a card, but work until 6.15 every evening except Sunday. By then all the shops are closed.

We had our maths exam yesterday and anti-gas this afternoon. I think I have just scraped through by the skin of my teeth in the maths, but the anti-gas was child's play. The results have not been announced yet. We started navigation yesterday in place of the usual maths period.

I should appreciate it if you would send the morse tapper as I could do with a spot of practice. In signalling we also use an Aldis lamp, the type seen flashing between destroyers and aircraft.

I did send a card to Mrs Randall and one to Aunty Bagnall and Miss Hanger. That ought to bring forth at least a scarf! It is bitterly cold today and we have had a fall of snow. Air raid warnings average about two a night. Never hear ack-ack or bombers. Have been having eye exercises for the last week and am assured that eyes will soon be A1.

Yours affectionately
Edwin

No. 2 Flight
No. 2 ITW
Pembroke College
Cambridge

11th January 1941

My dear Mother,

Thanks for the morse tapper and letter. I can now transmit at 6–8 words a minute and receive at 5–6. This morning we had two hours of morse and one hour of Aldis lamp, which was signalled by a corporal on the tower of a church 700 yards away.

I have some rather disappointing news to tell you. I did not pass the maths exam. Yesterday I was interviewed by a squadron leader. He says that I shall be given another chance, but it means another squadron and flight. I shall not leave Cambridge, but I shall lose all my friends. The reason I am getting another shot is that I am under military age and they can't re-muster me as a rear gunner unless I agree. Anyhow, we have all passed the anti-gas exam which was very simple.

You ask whether 10/–d a week will be enough money for me: I shall just try to make it last.

Malcolm and I always have a jolly good time on Sundays. Every Sunday since Boxing Day we have been to the Rudds to tea and supper. We always have a most enjoyable time there.

In answer to your query, there are about 1,000 of us here in Cambridge.

Yours affectionately
Edwin

No. 3 Flight
No. 2 ITW
Selwyn College
Cambridge

19th January 1941

My dear Mother,

As you can see I am now at Selwyn College. I will go through the whole course again with this new flight. There are two fellows here from the Argentine. One, with the surname of Wondham, knows Uncle Dudley and Aunt Gladys very well – and David Joyce is one of his best friends! He also knows cousins Honour and Joan and has been to parties at the house. He tells me that at the beginning of the war David volunteered to serve for three months guarding the Falkland Islands – and actually did so! Wondham says that David is now in Canada as an Under Training pilot.*

About the allowance again: I will go to the Pay Office on Tuesday (the only day it is open) and ask why you haven't received anything. I was only paid 24/–d this week, which means that the allowance has been deducted.

My old flight was issued with flying kit four days ago – and it is absolutely marvellous. I have seen Malcolm's.

So you have a shelter now!† I should think it must be rather chilly at night. I hope you are all well and safe what with all the raids and the snow. It has been pretty cold here in Cambridge and the Cam was frozen over this week, but not thick enough to allow skating.

Many kisses and love
Edwin

* David Joyce served in the RAF as a pilot and was killed in 1942. He was Edwin's cousin.

† This was a brick-built surface shelter with pre-cast concrete roof and a blast wall to shield the entrance, erected at the bottom of the garden and fitted with bunks.

No. 3 Flight
No. 2 ITW
Selwyn College
Cambridge

26th January 1941

My dear Mother,

On Tuesday and Thursday evenings I have extra practice after seven in signals and morse, and in the evenings on Monday, Wednesday and Friday I go to the Divinity College for maths tuition. We do all our work in the colleges – in Downing, Emmanuel, Selwyn, and occasionally for a clothing parade to Jesus.

Yesterday the medical Group Captain told me I had an unusual flaw in one eye, but with treatment it can be rectified. Later, Malcolm, Gerry and I had a wizard time: we went to the Rudd's for tea then with three of the daughters – Molly, Betty and Joan – and a friend, Sylvia, we went to a dance. Although this was only the second time I had ever danced, I danced with all the girls. Especially with Molly. She is 18 and the youngest. Malcolm is my rival – and he seems to have a bit of a lead. Mrs Rudd bought all the tickets at three shillings each. By RAF standards it was quite a swell affair! The place was filthy with pilot officers, observers and even some naval men. We were the only AC IIs [Aircraftmen Second Class] present. Mother, if David hasn't worn them out, will you please send me my brogues so I can dance a wee bit better than in my boots, newly shod all over with steel and iron!

I am worrying myself grey about the maths exam, which is due next Wednesday: I shall just have to do my best. During the past week my old flight have had exams every day: navigation, maths, hygiene, law and administration, aircraft and ship recognition, signals (morse and Aldis lamp) and armaments. Having passed all this they will become LACs and get 5/–d a day.

Last Thursday I had a psychological test. The object was to determine whether one is best suited for bombers or fighters. It is all very hush-hush. At the eye clinic they are testing fellows for night vision, selecting the best for night fighters.

About the five shillings, Mother. If I am to take Molly out, the cash would help considerably.

Affectionately
Edwin

A Flight
No. 4 Squadron
St John's College
Cambridge

12th February 1941

My dear Mother,

I arrived at Cambridge at 9.30 Sunday night after having spent a truly marvellous weekend at home. Thank you for making everything so enjoyable.

I sat for the maths exam today and I think I may say without any conceit that it is 'in the bag'.

Yesterday some Chinese generals inspected this ITW. Before they visited the cinema where we carry out aircraft recognition the CO instructed us: 'Even if you've seen the recognition film sixteen times for God's sake try to look interested and intelligent.'

Please don't worry about sending any chocolate, Mother, because I can usually get plenty in the NAAFI canteen: on the contrary, I can send you some.

Affectionately
Edwin

A Flight
No. 4 Squadron
St John's College
Cambridge

5th March 1941

My dear Mother,

My septic thumb is healing quite well. The MO gave me a whiff of gas and lanced the wretched thing then confined me to the Station Sick Quarters for three days. The Group Captain passed my eyes as completely 100% A1 fit!

Group HQ have been tightening up on exam passes: no second attempts are being allowed. Eleven fellows failed navigation last week and are re-mustering as wireless operator/air gunners.

I visited the Rudds with Malcolm last Sunday then went to a dance. We had a wizard time.

Affectionately
Edwin

A Flight
No. 4 Squadron
St John's College
Cambridge

15th March 1941

My dear Mother,

I was very pleased to hear from you – and the postal order was a Godsend as I have been on the rocks for days. Thanks again.

I have just had my thumb dressed and I have come into the Services Club in St Andrews Street to write this letter.

Last Thursday night Mr Rudd's daughters, Malcolm, Colin (a Sergeant pilot) and myself went to the RAF Comforts Show at the Guildhall. We saw Denny Dennis, Sam Costa and a jolly good band. Malcolm and I have also been to see an extremely funny Robertson Hare in <u>Women Aren't Angels</u> at the Arts Theatre.

Next week we are taking no less than 13 exams, all of which must be passed first time otherwise we shall forfeit our leave and have a very meagre chance of a second shot.

You were saying how beautiful the crocuses are in the garden, Mother. I wish you could see them in the college grounds. So many of them – all of different shades and colours, and the fine weather we have enjoyed makes Cambridge in the spring beautiful.

Affectionately
Edwin

A Flight
No. 4 Squadron
St John's College
Cambridge

4th April 1941

My dear Mother,

I arrived back safely and in good time last Sunday. The night was free from blitzes and I hope there haven't been any more severe raids at home.

All we fellows who failed the navigation exam were summoned before our CO last Tuesday evening. 'I have some good news for you,' he said. 'You are all to be given another chance.' We sat for the new exam today and I only hope I have managed to scrape up the 60%.

Malcolm has been taken off the overseas posting because his corrective flying goggles haven't come through. He's rather sick about it. So if I get through the navigation I stand a good chance of being posted with him.

This morning after the exam Williams and I did a stint of roof spotting on the top of St John's Chapel. It was rather fun – except for the journey up 194 steps. They are spiral, very dark and about three feet wide. The staircase is actually in one of the chapel pinnacles. Whilst I was on the roof Williams (a very keen photographer) snapped me twice with his super camera.

I enclose the ration money, Mother.

Affectionately
Edwin

A Flight
No. 4 Squadron
St John's College
Cambridge

Friday 7.10 12th April 1941

My dear Mother,

Congratulations Mother and Dad on your twenty-first wedding anniversary.

Now for the sad, sad news. Four of us out of the nine who sat for the navigation have failed and I am one of them. I do not know quite what will happen to us now.

Last Monday morning our Flight went on the range at the nearby EFTS and each was issued with twenty-five rounds of small arms ammunition. It was jolly good fun and by a bit of luck I managed to score two bulls eyes. After the firing we went into the EFTS canteen where fellows were sitting about in chairs in their flying kit waiting to go up. Lucky blighters! Twelve fellows from our Flight were posted to this EFTS last Wednesday and they were actually flying in the afternoon. They are having the time of their lives.

I am meeting Roley in the 'Baron of Beef' tonight for a farewell drink before he goes tomorrow: he has been waiting nine weeks to be posted.

The ration allowance money was for 15/–d, and as you have kindly suggested, Mother, I have bought myself 50 Players (3/9d) and will try and buy the book about the colleges tomorrow.

We have had an air raid warning four nights running in Cambridge.

I have seen two jolly good cinema shows this week. One of them was Gasbags and the other The Man Who Talked Too Much.

Affectionately
Edwin

A Flight
No. 4 Squadron
St John's College
Cambridge

19th April 1941

My dear Mother,

As regards sending me anything, Mother, I'm afraid I must have a spot of cash. I am in an awful hurry to catch the 3.30 post so please forgive the awful scribble.

I am so glad you are all safe after the heavy raid on Wednesday night. We only had a warning that night. No ack-ack, flares, bombs or anything. It does seem unfair.

Your affectionate (browned off)
Edwin

Magdalene College*
No. 2 ITW
Cambridge

27th April 1941

My dear Mother,

The Wing Commander said he could not possibly recommend me for another chance. He also said that as I am a volunteer I could have my discharge, re-muster as a wireless operator/air gunner or get a ground job in the RAF. Naturally I said I would go for WOP/AG. If I had my discharge I should only go into the army eventually – and I do want to make a go of it in the RAF.

You need have no fear about this re-mustering, Mother. A WOP/AG is not the rear gunner and he is as safe as the pilot. Furthermore, after having finished the WOP/AG course at Blackpool one is sometimes given the chance to re-muster back to pilot.

Of the others who failed the course, Amery asked for his discharge: another left to join the navy: and Wells has re-mustered with me. Until we are posted we shall do guard duties, fire picquets and fatigues – no lessons or lectures at all.

You cannot possibly imagine how impossible it is to exist on ten bob a week, Mother – after one visit to the cinema and 8d a day for something to eat. I really think I ought to have more. I used to be the only one in my old Flight who only drew £1 a fortnight instead of the full £1 14s. It was not only humiliating: the leg pulling was the worst. At the moment I am fed up to the teeth with the RAF and want to have a little money to try and keep up with my friends who are always buying me coffees, sandwiches and paying for the cinema seats.

Affectionately
Edwin

P. S. Tell anyone who ever enquires
        that as I failed the exam for pilot
        I have <u>volunteered</u> for WOP/AG.

* Founded 1542.

Magdalene College
No. 2 ITW
Cambridge

2nd May 1941

My dear Mother,

I am now really adjusted to the thought of becoming a WOP/AG and the prospects of good pay and promotion equally as good as those for pilot. The fully qualified WOP/AG's money has just been raised to 13/6d per day, the same as for a pilot or observer.

I shall do a purely wireless course at Blackpool lasting two months, become an LAC, and then go to Yatesbury in Wiltshire for the gunnery course.

I went to a show last Friday at the RAF Club, which included as a special guest artist Gordon Harker. He is currently appearing in a play by Richard Bird at the Arts Theatre called Once a Crook.

Tony Merritt who used to be in my old Flight at Selwyn invited me to a performance of the Sadler's Wells Opera Company's The Beggars Opera at the Arts. Earlier in the week they put on La Traviata and Figaro. Tony went to both. Probably because he went to the Newmarket races and backed a winner!

I have been trying to get some leave, but it is like trying to get blood from a turnip. But I've secured the promise of a long weekend – which is something.

Incidentally, Molly Rudd has enlisted in the Federated Ambulance Nursing Yeomanry (FANY to you!) She has to report to Aldershot on Monday week.

Affectionately
Edwin

It was a feature of the war that entertainers gave concerts or made personal appearances such as the one Edwin refers to at the RAF Club. Gordon Harker served in the forces but also engaged in public performances. He became one of the most popular of Britain's character actors and was the star of many movie classics right through the 30s and 40s. Critics referred to his warm humour, 'an artist with the common touch'. He endeared himself to the cinema-going public.

Jesus College
Cambridge

13th May 1941

My dear Mother,

Yesterday I was moved to Jesus, which is the headquarters of this ITW, and inevitably the discipline is very hot. My hitch-hiking was very successful for I arrived in Cambridge at 10 o'clock within fifty yards of Magdalene College. Thanks again for making my weekend so enjoyable, Mother. Isn't this Hess business a knockout?

Affectionately yours
Edwin

The Hess business which Edwin refers to as a 'knockout' was indeed a sensational and absurd act. No satisfactory answer has fully explained why the Führer's close aide Rudolph Hess deserted from an airfield near Munich in a Messerschmitt aircraft and landed in Renfrewshire in Scotland on 10 May 1941. Hess apparently hoped to open peace negotiations, but had not a chance of even getting such talks started. The misguided Nazi leader was locked up and treated as a prisoner of war.

After the war he was put on trial at Nuremberg with the other war criminals and imprisoned for life.

The question of Hess's sanity has never been satisfactorily resolved. The mystery of his mission and his odd behaviour have gone to the grave with him.

Jesus College
Cambridge

24th May 1941

My dear Mother,

I must apologise for not having answered your last letter sooner, but when I relate the stew I have been in you will realise that I haven't had much time to spare.

A week ago while on Fire Picquet Patrol another fellow and I were found in the canteen at 0040. We had just popped in to see the time and as we only had ten minutes left to patrol we stayed put! However, we were caught red handed by a flight sergeant who put us both under open arrest. We were charged in the morning by a squadron leader who awarded us 14 days CC. This CC business entails a lot of fatigues after the day's work is finished. I hope this news will not alarm you because it is really quite trivial. The charge was read like this: '1270671 Thomas E. G. Whilst on active service and on fire picquet was absent from duty from 0030 to 0040 hours.'

Thanks for the postal order. I will see the accounts about my pay next week.

Last Thursday evening I met a fellow, who came over to join up from Rio, another who came from China and another from Tahiti. The latter is Charles Mappin. He has met up with a Tahiti friend of his who is a pilot on a nearby aerodrome. The island, he tells me, only had ten Englishmen on it. I'm also told he's related to the Mappins of Mappin and Webb.

Your affectionate son
Edwin

P.S. CC in the RAF is known as Jankers.
Gerry Hall has finished the course at EFTS,
is now at SFTS and will have his wings in
6 weeks time. Malcolm is still unposted,
poor chap: he has been waiting 3½ months.

Jesus College
Cambridge

30th May 1941

My dear Mother,

Thank you very much for the parcel containing the pyjamas, biscuits and postal order. It was a pleasant surprise.

I have at last finished my jankers and have been invited by Betty, Joan and Malcolm to the theatre to celebrate. We are to see a comedy, <u>Miss Fitz-Newton</u>.

I have seen the accounts people and they will cancel the allowance – but it may take a month or so.

Wasn't the sinking of the <u>Bismarck</u> good news after the blowing up of the <u>Hood</u>?* We followed the chase very closely at Jesus and were thrilled.

Last Monday seven Stirlings flew over our college at a very low altitude. They flew in formation and looked simply magnificent. Since then I have seen one or two Manchesters and some Halifaxes cruising around.

Affectionately
Edwin

---

* The battle cruiser *Hood*, symbol of British supremacy at sea, was blown up in action with the German battle ship *Bismarck* in a dramatic encounter in the Atlantic. The Home Fleet and other naval units hunted and sank the *Bismarck*.

Edwin left Cambridge with many regrets for a posting to Blackpool to go on a wireless operator's course. With the adaptability of youth he adjusted readily to the new routines and environment.

84 Palatine Road
Blackpool
Lancs

11th July 1941

My dear Mother,

As you can see, I have changed my billet. The accommodation and atmosphere here are much better – and in the two days I have been here the food has been good.

I am having a perfectly marvellous time. The weather is grand and we swim regularly every night and at weekends.

As regards my birthday, I should very much like a tie and nylon toothbrush from the children. I would also like a pair of grey bags which I can buy when next on leave. This won't require any coupons because I can get a chit from the CO.

This course doesn't compare with the pilots' one. The morse is 'a piece of cake'. This afternoon we are to complete our rifle and bayonet course. The bayonet fighting – thrusting the bayonet into a sack – is good fun.

You'll be pleased to know that my disreputable uniform trousers have been condemned by the tailor and I shall be issued with a new pair tomorrow.

I am among a grand set of fellows. We share a number of billets in this road. We were all on the pilot's course and some had reached the EFTS before they pipped – mostly landings. One fellow named Baxter has a Sunbeam Talbot (a beaut) which we used to move all our kit bags when we changed billets.

Please convey my kindest regards to old Miss Bayford. You might explain to the old dame that there is a war on and there's a shortage of jam in Lancashire and tell her I'm crazy about her ... !

Affectionately yours
Edwin

84 Palatine Road
Blackpool
Lancs

20th July 1941

My dear Mother,

I should be grateful if you would hang on to my bags until I get some leave. Did you manage to get them without coupons, or shouldn't I ask?

I am due for my seven words per minute test in morse tomorrow. We increase the speed by one word per week. We go up to tens and then should have one week's leave.

I wonder if you'd like me to send some chocolate to you – e.g. 2½d Cadbury's fruit and nut, crisps, ration choc? Please let me know because I can get a nice little stack over a period of seven days.

I saw the musical <u>Lady Behave</u> last Monday. Sally Gray and Pat Kirkwood were charming and Stanley Lupino as funny as ever. This is the first show he has presented in Blackpool: it has already appeared in Manchester and will end up in the West End.

I have an interesting week ahead of me. I am going to see the film <u>Dear Brutus</u>, starring John Gielgud, Muriel Pavlow and Roger Livesy. I am going to the theatre and the gang say they are going to get me tight on my birthday on Wednesday. And on Tuesday I am meeting Cathleen.

Tons of hugs and kisses.

Affectionately
Edwin

84 Palatine Road
Blackpool
Lancs

25th July 1941

My dear Mother,

Thanks for the goodies – especially the chocolate cakes, the cigarette and tobacco: and please thank Dad for the PO which was most welcome. The writing pad is first class.

The whole gang went on a binge on my birthday: Stanley, Stinker, Baxter (wee Scotsman, ex-Corporal Gordon Highlanders) and Ronnie Wells plus two girls who are holiday-making and are staying in Stanley's billet. I'm afraid we all had too much to drink.

I am getting on well with the course. We have four hours a day of morse.

There is a Scotsman in the billet who is carving me a ring from a piece of the perspex windscreen of a Whitley bomber which crashed on returning from a bombing raid on Germany.

Thanks again for everything.

Your loving son
Edwin

1270588 Malcolm
No. 29 Course
12 SFTS
Grantham

9th August 1941

My dear old Edwin,

How grand it was to hear from you. You are certainly working up to a ferocious speed at morse and I suppose it won't be long before you're a fully fledged WOP/AG. It must be good to have all those blokes up there.

I suppose you might like to hear how things are going at my end of the globe. I was posted – eventually – to No. 17 EFTS, North Luffenham. Half way through the course they bunged us out to make way for a bomber squadron. We finished the EFTS course at Peterborough and went straight on to this place without leave or anything. It took yours truly a whole ten hours to go solo on Tigers, and four hours on Oxfords. I've given up the idea of single-engined fighters and am having a terrific crack at Coastal Command. But a lot will depend upon the wings exam in five weeks time.

We ought to try and get to OTU together, you know. We could if we made special application through the proper channels.

It's an awful lot of piffle what people say about the AO being a dangerous aeroplane. It is rather like an organ with bags of levers etc. and two socking great throttles! They are absolute bug bears to land because the tail won't go down properly and it drifts for miles before touching down. But I mustn't talk shop – it sounds so bad. But if we can get on ops together, we will shake those German swine!

At the moment I am in a state of breathless and uncontrollable excitement because tomorrow (my half day) I am going to visit a certain university town where my little sweetheart is also spending the weekend. Oh boy! It's such a blazes of a time since I saw her.

I miss you like anything, you know, Edwin, and I don't think I'll find a friend to replace you in this service. All the original friends have gone. Gerry, by the way, is a be-winged fighter sergeant pilot. Do you remember John Orr who was at Pembroke with us? He has just passed his wings exam on the senior course here, training on Ansons, the jammiest kites in the service. Anyway, he asks to be remembered to you. The only other bloke I've seen recently is Charlie Doadkin who failed the course at Luffenham and re-mustered as an observer.

My best wishes to any of the lads up there, and the same a hundred times over to yourself. See you soon, maybe over Berlin, if not before.

Cheerio, old man, and all the best,

Yours as ever,
Malcolm

56 Charnley Road
Blackpool
Lancs

22nd August 1941

My dear Mother,

I have changed my address once again. I kicked up such a fuss in the Squadron Office: in typical RAF style they didn't investigate the complaint, they simply moved me. This billet is fine – and it is nearer the parade ground where we parade at 7.30 each morning.

I have 'passed out' on the course here and am now awaiting posting. I got an 'A' category in all of my tests at ten words per minute: only twelve from thirty-two achieved this.

On Monday night we are to have a celebration. I would like to ask if you could send me a postal order for 7/6d. I shall be able to pay you back in full when I come home on leave. I didn't want to celebrate particularly, but the gang wouldn't take no for an answer.

I was specially pleased to receive the letter from Malcolm. Look at a picture of an AO then realise that Malcolm is only 18½ and is flying these crates!

I saw the film <u>Fantasia</u> last week. I specially went for the music, and it really is grand – especially the scene where Disney depicts elephants, ostriches, rhinoceroses and crocodiles to the ballet music <u>Dance of the Hours</u>. This scene is the funniest and the music the most inspiring. It ended far too soon.

Your affectionate
Edwin

A telegram from Edwin to his mother:

> TO MRS E. G. THOMAS 38 HIGHSTONE AVENUE
> WANSTEAD ESSEX = A BOY COMING HOME ON
> LEAVE ARRIVING TOMORROW = LOVE = EDWIN

There is no date for this telegram from Edwin to his mother. The light-hearted wording indicates an eagerness to get home and enjoy the warmth and comfort of the family. Edwin was quick to take advantage of any leave offered, however short, and in spite of air raids.

The RAF was gradually growing in strength and the military targets in Germany were getting repeated assaults. By now, too, the major strategy of the war had taken a dramatic turn with German armies invading Russia, leading to some of the mightiest land battles.

Hut Z30
3 Wing
B Squadron
RAF Station
Yatesbury
Wilts

12th September 1941

My dear Mother,

I have only been in this camp about an hour so know little about it yet. My hut houses about thirty beds and a wireless set. We seem to be in the middle of the country about four miles from Calne. The camp itself is huge and seems to consist of nothing but huts – large and small. There is a cinema, a NAAFI and a YMCA so the fellows rarely leave the camp. I met a Cambridge fellow who had been here two weeks and he's only been out of the camp once.

We are short of cigarettes. We are given a ticket which entitles us to buy twenty a week. If you will please send me a few, Mother, I will send you a PO.

The radio works: and now fellows are lazing on their beds, reading, writing letters or playing cards.

The NCO in charge has warned us that next week we shall all be on duty each evening after seven as a defence precaution and to familiarise ourselves with our duties in case of attack.

The course here lasts twelve weeks – after which we should get a week's leave. We then go on another course for two or three months and then return here for a refresher which can last anything up to six weeks. Only then will we go on our air gunnery course of six weeks. So you can see, Hitler has nothing to fear until the end of May 1942.

We were all heartened when we arrived here to see the sky crammed full of aircraft of every description some of which were landing in the field adjoining the camp. But our hopes of flying have been dispelled: flying for WOP/AGs under training was cut out recently. Those who are flying all seem to be Australians who completed their course at home but seem to need refreshing now.

Thank you again for a lovely leave.

Love to all.

Affectionately
Edwin

Hut Z30
B Squadron
3 Wing
RAF Station
Yatesbury
Wilts

21st September 1941

My dear Mother,

Now that I have been here nine days I have settled down and am working hard. I am very comfortable: the food is good and plentiful – and the NAAFI well stocked.

I successfully passed our elevens test with an 'A'. We are learning a good deal of the technical side of both wireless and electricity. It's all rather confusing at first but one picks it up gradually.

As well as attaining a speed of eighteens in morse we have to pass out at eights in Aldis lamps which should be easy: plus some standard at semaphore. We work every day except Sunday from 8 until 5.30. On Thursday afternoons there are a variety of sports to play including cycling, fencing, baseball and even open air swimming.

In the evenings, after reading a few chapters of Negley Farson's <u>The Way of a Transgressor</u> I trot round to the NAAFI with the boys where we drink NAAFI tea and enjoy long talks on politics.

I had my teeth examined yesterday and the dentist was surprised at the quality of the dentistry.

I have to report to our Flight Sergeant because a friend and I were caught in No. 2 Wing's NAAFI. I am sure I shall be able to convince him of my ignorance of the rules regarding canteens.

Affectionately
Edwin

Hut Z30
B Squadron
3 Wing
RAF Yatesbury
Wilts

14th October 1941

My dear Mother,

I have to take my fifteens in morse one day this week. At every test we seem to panic more than ever, but with luck I should get an 'A' or at worst a 'B' —which isn't frowned upon. Since I have been back I have been working on a five valve receiver and transmitter.

When we finish this course and earn our 'sparks' badge we will be granted FOURTEEN DAYS leave!! We are due to pass out on December 5th and will therefore have to return to our new station a week before Christmas Day.

The new CO ordered a kit inspection on Thursday. When we had finished our sports afternoon we had to lay out our kit in regulation fashion: a job that entails cleaning about 24 buttons and two pairs of boots. While we spent two hours on the job, the CO was in and out of the hut in four minutes having inspected thirty-five beds, men and kits.

After having been on parade every evening at seven for the last seven days, last night we endured a hut inspection, standing by our beds yet again after having scrubbed and polished the hut. So tonight is my first free evening in nine days. I'm not moaning about it all: I simply thought you might like to have an insight into the daily life of an AC2 in Yatesbury!

Your affectionate son
Edwin

Hut Z30
B Squadron
3 Wing
RAF Yatesbury
Wilts

23rd October 1941

My dear Mother,

It has been rather an eventful day. This morning we were all summoned from our classes and paraded, then lined the route in the perishing cold for an hour. The King drove by followed by other cars with notables: he alighted and inspected one of the classrooms. We all had a good view of him in his Air Force uniform.

Your affectionate son
Edwin

Hut Z30
B Squadron
3 Wing
RAF Yatesbury
Wilts

31st October 1941

My dear Mother,

It has been very cold here. Last Wednesday we had some snow – but hardly enough to cover the camp. As for the wind, it simply blows a gale.

Yesterday we had our sixteens test and I passed with an 'A'. I am also progressing quite well with the transmitter and receiver sets.

I am enclosing the debt I owe and want to thank you for the loan and for the marvellous weekend.

Affectionately yours
Edwin

Hut Z30
B Squadron
3 Wing
RAF Yatesbury
Wilts

9th November 1941

My dear Mother,

I have a pass this weekend and intend visiting Bath with a few of the chaps. We will arrive at about seven, bag a bed in the YMCA for a bob and go to a show in the evening. And on Sunday we can visit the famous suspension bridge high across the Avon.

I've enjoyed working on a new transmitter/receiver this week, similar to the set you saw in the film The Lion Has Wings. No morse is transmitted on an R/T set: only speech – radio telephony. My call sign was Primrose and the station I had to tune into and transmit to was Leopard. The chap at Leopard reminded me of Gordon Harker: he is a mimic, a cockney, and against all the regulations used his time on the 'air' telling jokes, impersonating people and singing. In Civvy Street he robbed gas meters in disused houses.

After the reports of all our losses in raids on Berlin and Cologne there is much jovial talk of re-mustering for pilots …

I had fun last Wednesday night at our Wing Dance which Tony and I gate-crashed. We buttonholed a cross-eyed LAC who was standing outside the NAAFI canteen, and he advised us to try to make our entry by a door at the back of the building marked 'Corporals'. We took his advice but the door wouldn't budge an inch. We battered at the bally thing for ages then it finally 'gave' with a noise that seemed almost to bring the building down. It had been held fast with a chair. We entered a small room in pitch darkness, barking our shins, laughing and crashing into one another. We found another door leading into the Sergeants Cloakroom. We plucked up courage, put on a bold front and simply walked through into the dance hall. Of course, most of the Waafs were bagged by then … but we enjoyed ourselves. We drank cider and NAAFI beer. The latter is as flat as a pancake, and doesn't deserve the name beer.

Yours affectionately
Edwin

Hut Z30
B Squadron
3 Wing
RAF Yatesbury
Wilts

17th November 1941

My dear Mother,

Five of us had a jolly good time in Bristol. We saw Brunel's marvellous piece of engineering 750ft high across the Avon. Quite a breath-taking experience which I shall never forget. We visited the Zoological Gardens. As we walked past some ravens my friend and I heard someone say 'Hello!' We looked at each other then realised neither had spoken. It was a raven.

I continue to do well in my regular tests having scored three 'As' recently.

Your affectionate son
Edwin

Hut Z30
B Squadron
3 Wing
RAF Yatesbury
Wilts

23rd November 1941

My dear Mother,

Thanks for the parcel. The collars are very welcome: the pipe is as sweet as sugar, the tobacco delicious and the chewing gum sustaining.

Regarding another smack at pilot: I was interviewed by the CO last week but all I could get out of him was that I must apply at my next station. This, of course, is the standard non-committal reply. I have decided to have a word with the padre and seek his advice. He is the man we all turn to when we get little or no satisfaction elsewhere.

Had rather a good game of hockey last Thursday after-noon. I was selected for the 1st XI. We drew two all, most of the credit being due to two of our forwards, both WOP/AG Aussies who played very well, were as keen as mustard and shouted instructive remarks to all and sundry.

I have recently read the HMSO booklet entitled <u>Bomber Command</u>. Do read it. It reconstructs some of the earliest of our raids beginning with the dropping of leaflets and it gives a good insight into the duties of pilot, navigator and WOP/AG in action.

It was sad to hear of the sinking of the <u>Ark Royal</u>* – especially was this so for one of our instructors whose son is an observer in the Fleet Air Arm aboard the <u>Ark</u>. He has another son who has just earned his wings in the RAF.

Your affectionate son
Edwin

* The aircraft carrier *Ark Royal* foundered off Gibraltar on 14 November 1941 after being torpedoed by a U-boat.

Hut Z30
B Squadron
3 Wing
RAF Yatesbury
Wilts

7th December 1941

My dear Mother,

You must forgive me for not having written earlier but I have been binding for our exams. All have been passed happily enough, except for one more to be taken next week. It now looks as if I shall be posted on 18th or 19th December. So it means Christmas at home!

We are back in our own dining hall again – where they know how to cook. Two dining halls serve our squadron: so it isn't so very difficult to have two meals! I had two good dinners today.

I am much envied these days. I have a pair of flying boots which I'm afraid I swank about in.

We have just heard a variety programme on the wireless: the rest of the fellows are resting, sleeping, writing letters or 'binding' among themselves, although most of the fellows have gone away for the week ... ah! ... but I shall be home for Christmas.

Your affectionate son
Edwin

Curiously Edwin makes no reference in his letters home to one of the greatest events in the war – the Japanese attack on Pearl Harbor early in December 1941. The great news he announced in his letter of 16 December was the granting of eleven days leave – Home for Christmas!

Hut Z30
B Squadron
3 Wing
RAF Yatesbury
Wilts

16th December 1941

My dear Mother,

I have some great news! I have passed my final Board and have just sewn on my sparks badge! Better news to come … I am leaving here on Friday 19th for eleven days leave!

I was first of the 28 to go before the Board. The tests were quite straightforward, really – and made so by the great amount of practice we've had in the past few weeks. Three fellows failed, including one from the Argentine, who made matters worse by swearing at the flight sergeant when given the news.

It is ironic that now we are classed as tradesmen we are engaged in 'jankers' work all day – scrubbing and polishing floors, digging allotments close by the main road enduring insults and jeers from passing army convoys.

The letter you re-addressed to me was from Molly Rudd giving the news that Malcolm was at her home a month ago showing off his wings.

The main attraction in the ENSA concert tonight in the camp theatre is George Formby. Tomorrow night we are all going on a binge to celebrate the end of the course – and I expect it will end with a terrific pillow fight about eleven o'clock.

Your affectionate son
Edwin

SHQ Signals
Hut 172
Frinningham
RAF Station
Detling
Kent

31st December 1941

My dear Mother,

I arrived safely at this station yesterday – and what a place it is! There is no electric light in the huts. We have oil lamps and a peculiar heater at one end. To wash we do the best we can from a bin full of water by the doorway.

But worst of all, the hut is a mile from our signal room amid a dense wood.

There are no planes here and the camp appears to be spread-eagled across the countryside perched atop a hill – 700 feet above sea level. My first impression on arrival was that I was joining a lumber camp. Our hut is wonderfully camouflaged by trees which completely obscure the old shack. When you wake in the morning you see wisps of branches hitting the windows. So dense is the forest that engineers working on a construction job only a hundred yards away can't be seen.

The camp had an awful shaking a year ago when Jerry knocked out a number of buildings including the theatre and the cinema which still haven't been rebuilt.

Tomorrow I start work at 7.30 and finish at midday. Then I go on watch again at 10.30pm till 7.30 the next morning – and so on without respite! The chances of re-mustering from here appear to be pretty slim and the prospect of three or four months here is enough to shake me.

We have our meals in a little shack made quaint by a crooked little chimney from which the smoke floats up towards the treetops.

We have a fellow in the hut called Bob Ashley who was a singer with Jack Payne's band. It is he who owns the radio in the hut – which has just been switched on for a comedy programme with Gillie Potter.

The operational signal HQ where I work is quite an intriguing place. It is a concrete construction just showing above ground with one or two large pylons nearby. It is camouflaged by netting with lots of grass strewn over it. It is supposed to be air conditioned.

Apologies for this miserable letter, darling: but don't worry, I am doing all I can to re-muster and get out of here – or desert! Write soon.

Your affectionate son
Edwin

SHQ Signals
Detling
nr Maidstone
Kent

9 January 1942

My dear Mother,

So pleased to receive a letter from you all and am glad to say I am considerably less cheesed than when I wrote last.

A few days ago when I stepped out of the transmitting station at Cold Blow in the pitch dark I walked into a trench of water which lapped round my knees. I extricated myself all right and squelched the mile back to my hut.

Then last night – coming off duty at 10.30 in the blackness – I lost myself. The route home from the transmitting station at Cold Blow (my goodness it blows cold here at 700ft above sea level) lies across a ploughed field, then across another field of grazing pasture land. The weather was cold, foggy, as well as pitch dark – and silent. So very eerie! I lost my direction half way across the ploughed field and managed to reach the hut safely after climbing through barbed wire, none the worse for my little blunder.

What a cold spot this is! All that eye-wash about Kent being the Garden of Eden may be all right in spring with the apple orchards and hop fields but now it reminds me of the wilder parts of the Yorkshire moors, and in other parts of a lumber camp in the Rockies!

A number of us went to Maidstone to see the film <u>The 49th Parallel</u> which has been the talk of the camp. One Canadian corporal has seen it three times already.

Your affectionate son
Edwin

The 49th Parallel was a taut, suspenseful World War II drama film about a party of Nazi servicemen, survivors of the sinking of their U-boat, trying to land on American soil – still at that time neutral – and it follows their adventures in gripping detail. The trouble was that the natural heroes of the film were the Nazis. The film was strongly criticised for its sympathetic portrayal of the Nazis at a time when U-boats were sinking merchant ships in the Battle of the Atlantic. The main film stars of the film were Eric Portman, Laurence Olivier, Leslie Howard and Raymond Massey.

SHQ Signals
RAF Detling
nr Maidstone
Kent

15th January 1942

My dear Mother,

I am on duty in the transmitting station at Cold Blow, in the middle of a field now covered with quite a heavy fall of snow – with a piercingly cold wind. I am alone apart from a mechanic to service the sets in case of breakdown, and numerous guards to defend this shack. Every day we get more accustomed to this camp, but the irregular hours are tiresome. Half the time we don't know what day it is.

Your affectionate son
Edwin

Sergeant Wireless Operator/Air Gunner Edwin G. Thomas RAFVR.

Edwin, aged about eight, with his younger brother David
and his sister Margaret in São Paulo.

By the sea at Cliftonville, about 1938.

Training in 1941: Edwin aged twenty.

Bomber aircrew carried small passport-sized photographs for false identity
cards in occupied Europe. Note the blacked-out V-neck pullover.

SERGEANTS' MESS,

ROYAL AIR FORCE STATION, HARWELL, DIDCOT,

BERKS.

Hampstead Norris,
Nr. Newbury,
Berks. 19/x/42.

My dear Mother,

Thank you for your letter
received yesterday. I was sorry to hear of your
cold and hope you are feeling a little more
like yourself. The weather here has been very
cold but with very little rain.

I heard the "Victory Bells" last Sunday in
the old historic town of Bath! The whole affair
was rather curious. Last Saturday morning we
were up on a three hour cross. flying in
putrid weather. When we returned to base
we just saw a mass of grey where we thought
the 'drome was! However we were diverted
to another 'drome (one of our satellites, by
wireless) and found the sun shining there and
managed to get down O.K.

On arrival there we found two of our own
planes who had also landed. After a while we

A typical page from one of the many letters.

NEWS OF THE WORLD. April 18, 1943

Your Nose filters the air you breathe. Keep it clear and you stand a much better chance of avoiding Catarrh. To relieve congestion and soothe irritation use "Mentholatum." Insert a little of this breathable balm in the nostrils. Its pleasant aromatic vapours o-p-e-n up your Nose, clear your head, end Catarrh and Cold troubles. All Chemists 7d. & 1/3. Also in Liquid form 1/5 inc. tax.

MENTHOLATUM

No. 5,190 [Estab. 1843]   Registered at the General Post Office as a Newspaper   Telephones: Central 3030   SUND

Certified Net Sale Excee

HITLER'S ARSENAL

We Lost 55 'Planes, but Skoda was 'A

TERRIFIC CLIMAX TO
100 HOURS OF
NON-STOP BOMBING

HONOURABLE LIA
APPEAL TO ME FC
AFTER SAYING E
EMPIRE WAS CRU
TO PIECES

FROM preliminary details available last night it is pretty certain that the mammoth attack by the R.A.F. on Pilsen in Czecho-Slovakia in the early hours of yesterday completely destroyed a great part of the famous Skoda Armament Works.

In London the raid is already assessed as "a major German defeat," and an outstanding example of Bomber Command's determination to blast Hitler's mighty arsenals out of the war.

This devastating descent on Pilsen and a simultaneous attack on Mannheim in the Rhineland rounded off 100 hours of non-stop bombing by the Royal Air Force and their American colleagues.

Out of a total force of more than 600 heavy bombers, carrying possibly 1,500 tons of high explosives and incendiaries, we lost 37 in the Pilsen raid and 18 at Mannheim—our greatest aggregate of the war to date.

seems to have taken the Germans by surprise.

Crews agree that the flak was only moderate and the searchlights were so few that they could be counted.

HAZARDS COMING HOME

But along the route fighters were up in numbers.

The night was still almost as clear as day when the bombers were coming home, and with the moon overhead our pilots had to pass through several belts of defences, including the now notorious one in the Rhineland.

Flight-Sergt. Clifford Schnier flew through what he called "a wicked section of flak, searchlights, muck, and corruption."

"We had no alternative but to try to fight our way through it," he said.

"As we were flying through the flak we were picked up by a blue cone of searchlights. I lowered my seat and tried to stick my head down into the cockpit. Even there the light was absolutely blinding.

"Suddenly it turned from blue to white, and the fuselage was filled with it

Forts S

Plant

16 LOST:

SHO

BOMBER COMMAND SETS
UP A NEW RECORD

THE twin attack on Pilsen and Mannheim marked a new peak in

early pilots, " the flares went down and we could see individual factory buildings standing out quite clearly. My bomb-aimer had them filled with it

WITHIN a few of the return c R.A.F. bombers

This Sunday newspaper front page carried the story of the operations to Pilsen and Mannheim on the night of 16/17 April 1943.

This scroll commemorates

Sergeant E. G. Thomas
Royal Air Force

held in honour as one who
served King and Country in
the world war of 1939-1945
and gave his life to save
mankind from tyranny. May
his sacrifice help to bring
the peace and freedom for
which he died.

Edwin's commemorative scroll.

The Airmen's Memorial in
York Minster.

Roye Cemetery in France and Edwin's grave.

SHQ Signals
RAF Detling
nr Maidstone
Kent

[undated]

My dear Mother,

I arrived back in camp safe, sound and with time to spare on Monday. It was lovely to be home – if only to feel warm! The weather here is colder than ever – but already there is the prospect of another weekend pass – so please expect me this Saturday.

Your affectionate son
Edwin

SHQ Signals
RAF Detling
nr Maidstone
Kent

3rd February 1942

My dear Mother,

Last Friday we were called to action stations at 5am. We were ordered from our dugouts to collect a box of grenades. The fellow carrying the box dropped the lot. The lid flew off and twelve grenades scuttled all over the concrete floor. None exploded!

Your affectionate son
Edwin

SHQ Signals
RAF Station
Detling
nr Maidstone
Kent

14th February 1942

My dear Mother

Thank you again for a lovely 48. Conditions have improved. We have now been supplied with electricity! And the mild weather has improved our attitudes.

I was watching a number of Spitfires the other day. They are almost obsolete nowadays and are used almost exclusively as recce planes, carrying one large camera mounted beneath the fuselage – and no armaments. The pilots were wearing no flying kit – just parachute harness and helmet.

I met a naval fellow at a dance the other night, a 20 year old Sub-Lieutenant. I asked him which ship he was in and he replied 'the Sheffield'. I asked him what class of ship she was and he replied 'I can see you don't read the papers: she's a cruiser.'* He asked all about the air gunners course because he was trying to get a transfer. I tried all I could to dissuade him but it only seemed to make him keener!

Affectionately yours
Edwin

* The cruiser *Sheffield* had participated in the chase of the *Bismarck* some months earlier in May 1941.

SHQ Signals
RAF Detling
nr Maidstone
Kent

15 March 1942

My dear Mother

Bob and I hitch-hiked into town yesterday afternoon in a luxurious Rover to discover on arrival that it was Warship Week. A procession through the streets included members of the forces and civilian defence workers. A squadron of aircraft flashed by and were gone in seconds. The town had quite a carnival atmosphere.

One of the large motor car showrooms staged an exhibition of naval and military items including a Tiger Moth, a revolving gun turret, diving suits and a sea mine. The town had adopted the week enthusiastically, presumably because the great naval port of Chatham is only ten miles or so away – and the town is plastered with posters and photographs of naval craft. Dances, whist drives and football matches have been arranged.

We had toast, jam, tea and cakes in a little-known tea room: what a change from the awful food we have at the camp.

We returned by ten for our turn of watch: as ridiculous as ever with thirteen men on duty to man two radio sets: off duty at 2am, in bed at three, up for breakfast, back to bed till dinner, then back on duty at 12.30.

Now here I am writing this on a sunny Sunday afternoon. The weather has been pleasant for the past two weeks and the bluebell shoots are just visible poking through the ground outside our hut.

Yours affectionately
Edwin

SHQ Signals
RAF Detling
nr Maidstone
Kent

2nd April 1942

My dear Mother,

I have had to report to the Station Sick Quarters each day for ointment treatment for a rash on my face, and afterwards I rest in the warm sunshine amid lovely scenery. From my vantage point high above the camp one has a beautiful view of the north Downs and basking there gazing at such serenity I find it difficult to realise that men are at war.

I am writing this letter in the midst of one of our panic invasion scares. The whole camp is mobilised and in a state of readiness to deal out death to the enemy. I shouldn't care to be a Jerry parachutist! The whole affair lasts about 24 hours and browns every airman off to a cinder.

Your affectionate son
Edwin

SHQ Signals
RAF Detling
nr Maidstone
Kent

9th April 1942

My dear Mother,

I arrived back safely last night: another friend and I have just eaten the whole of your cake between us!

Today I was tried before the CO on two charges. The first related to four of us turning up late on watch – which was happily explained away because we hadn't been called in good time. The other charge was trivial and earned a simple admonition.

The <u>Sheffield</u> naval officer has invited me to his twenty-first birthday celebration. He tells me he has passed a medical for the RAF and is anxious to make the changeover. He complained that as a Sub-Lieutenant he was getting only nine bob a day – which is paltry compared with RAF ops men.

Love
Edwin

SHQ Signals
RAF Detling
nr Maidstone
Kent

21st April 1942

My dear Mother,

Just a short note to let you know I shall be home on Friday for a three day pass.

I had a flip in an Anson this afternoon. It was only a brief trip because once we were up the weather became very misty and flying was cancelled. The weather for the past few days has been really beautiful – so glorious that all my cares have gone!

Continuing our ground defence programme of training – tonight at ten we are going on night manoeuvres ... crawling around in the moonlight. I don't relish the thought of someone prowling around two feet away from me in the dark with a fixed bayonet.

Yours affectionately
Edwin

No. 2 AACU
RAF Detling
nr Maidstone
Kent

17th May 1942

My dear Mother,

You will see from the above address that I have left Signals. I have been 'loaned out' with five friends to act as operators in Battle aircraft. The plane is fitted with a drogue* towed astern as an anti-aircraft target. We take off, head across the Thames estuary for Sheerness where the naval gunners fire off at the drogue. So far I have been here nine days – but have not gone aloft yet! As compensation we have been issued with flying battle-dress – but are not allowed to wear it outside camp.

I had a glorious flight last week: a three hour trip in a gun turret to Birmingham and back. Wizard!

The weather today is really great and the walk to church this morning was very pleasant so I am going for a walk now to enjoy it all the more.

Affectionately
Edwin

* Drogue: a wind sock towed astern from an aircraft as a target for training gunners.

No. 2 AACU
RAF Detling
nr Maidstone
Kent

30th May 1942

My dear Mother

There is little fear of the AA blokes hitting <u>me</u>. Reason 1: I haven't been up yet! Reason 2: the drogue is let out to 5,000 to 7,000 feet on a wire, depending upon the dash of the pilot.

Your affectionate son
Edwin

No. 2 AACU
RAF Detling
nr Maidstone
Kent

14th June 1942

My dear Mother

I arrived back safely despite forgetting to change at Strood, and finished the journey at Chatham instead of Maidstone. After waiting a good time for a bus I arrived at Maidstone to discover the last one had gone. As I was in no rush to reach camp until early the next morning I shared a room with a sailor in a private house! The sailor had just returned from sea having been away for eleven months. He had a fund of interesting yarns.

I have practically given up hope of being a drogue operator and console myself with pulling away the chocks and spinning the propellors of aircraft!

Your affectionate son
Edwin

D Squadron
Air Crew Wing
RAF Madley
Herefordshire

29th June 1942

My dear Mother,

Arrived at this new station safely. Great news. The course here lasts only four or five weeks then straight on to gunnery. The food is good, the huts comfortable and I have met a lot of my old friends.

The nearest town – Hereford – is 9 miles distant. The discipline here is non-existent. Which makes us all very happy. Please forgive the postcard.

Your affectionate son
Edwin

A greetings telegram from Edwin sent on 6 July 1942:

GREETINGS MRS THOMAS 38 HIGHSTONE AVENUE WANSTEAD
ESSEX MANY HAPPY RETURNS OF TODAY ALL LOVE FROM EDWIN

No. 1 Air Crew Wing
D Squadron
RAF Madley
nr Hereford

11th July 1942

My dear Mother,

I am getting some flying hours in at last. Last Wednesday we flew to the Bristol Channel and yesterday over the mountainous Welsh border. It was rather fun flying through solid cloud then emerging into brilliant sunshine. I have only one more exercise to complete in these two-engined kites, then transfer to single-engined: it has all been easy so far – 'a piece of cake'.

We've been taking advantage of the lovely weather during the past few days and I am feeling fit, possibly because we play the Canadian national sport of Soft Ball – a combination of rounders and baseball. The Canadians here certainly show us a thing or two.

Your affectionate son
Edwin

No. 1 Air Crew Wing
D Squadron
RAF Madley
nr Hereford

26th July 1942

My dear Mother,

Your lovely parcel reminded me it was my twentieth birthday!

We are due to pass out this week and should be posted to gunnery, but there are some horrible rumours that the course is to be lengthened by four weeks. Several fellows have been posted here whom I knew at Detling and we enjoy talking about that comic station. I also met our Cambridge drill instructor, a flight sergeant. I saw him standing in a bus queue. He recalled cutting my hair – and remarked I could do with another cut.

I had rather a wizard time at the Royal Ordnance Factory dance last Tuesday which was held to aid the Russia Fund. It is the best ballroom for miles around here and I stayed until the end – midnight.

I was flying last Friday, again this morning and shall be flying again tomorrow morning: parade at 7.10am! I have found the exercises well within my scope and now rather enjoy the transfer from a crowded 'twin' to a plane with just the pilot and myself. On Friday I had an Indian pilot and for the second flight a Pole. It has been rather bumpy lately, with the aircraft falling twenty feet without warning just as the poor WOP is trying to tune in to base by moving a delicate control a fraction. This morning it was like a bus ride.

The camp is in the heart of the country, surrounded by apple orchards. During our break in the afternoon's morse practices we hop over the fence and bag a few apples each. During the last week the farmers have employed students as labourers. They are very sympathetic to us and fill our hats with raspberries. But yesterday I was unlucky. About 48 of us nipped smartly over the barbed wire entanglements to go scrumping, filling our blouses with apples. But I didn't see them scatter on the approach of a farmer. I made good my escape with another fellow – re-entered the camp site munching an apple – and was stopped by an SP

Flight Sergeant. I gave him my name and number and Wing – but not my squadron so perhaps no charges will be made.

If anyone knows the lyrics for <u>Blues in the Night</u> I'd like them. And the next time you write to Eddie Goddard in Germany please give him my regards.

Your affectionate son
Edwin

No. 1 Air Crew Wing
D Squadron
RAF Madley
nr Hereford

16th August 1942

My dear Mother,

Thank you for the parcel containing the pullovers: since receiving them the weather has changed and today the sun is shining brilliantly. Great news: I had my final Board this morning and am confident I have passed.

Last Friday the gang celebrated our impending departure with a dance at the ROF Hostel. Our partners were girls who work all day with gunpowder rather than face powder. I missed the last bus home but managed to get a taxi for the six mile trip back to camp: having resigned myself to the long walk back I went to the refreshment bar and met an old friend from a firm of registrars in Moorgate.

I am looking forward to the gunnery course. By the time I complete it I shall have been in the service two years. Incredible!

Your affectionate son
Edwin

Hut 194
T Wing
RAF Evanton
Ross-shire

23rd August 1942

My dear Mother,

I have arrived safely in Bonnie Scotland and find the camp rather good. But now I find I shall need the rest of my flying kit, so will you please send it as quickly as possible to this address.

I have just started the course at 1.30 this afternoon – Sunday! I expect to be here four weeks and to start air firing next week.

The journey from Hereford last week lasted nineteen hours. We are as far from London as Berlin is from parts of England.

The camp is cosmopolitan for we have Czechs, Poles, Norwegians, Scots, Englishmen and Welshmen. Happily we all get along quite well. Most of the fellows in my squad are excited because they have just been issued with their aircrew battle dress.

Please forgive this very short note, Mother, but I have a heck of a lot to do: we have only just finished the afternoon work – and it is 6.30. We shall all have to work very hard here.

Your affectionate son
Edwin

Hut 194
T Wing
RAF Evanton
Ross-shire

29th August 1942

My dear Mother,

We have had many lectures on guns, turrets, pyrotechnics, 'ditching' drill, hydraulics, sighting. We do no wireless work at all, for which we are grateful.

All the Scottish papers have given great prominence to the Duke of Kent's air crash,* and indeed the Sunderland crashed in this area. The boys who have been flying have kept a sharp lookout for it but so far haven't spotted it.

Three of our boys had an exciting time one day this week. When out over the North Sea an engine cut and they had to ditch. They were lucky: the water was only five feet deep. Had they landed in deeper water they would have gone through the ditching drill, knocked out the dinghy and floated with their Mae Wests which we are compelled to wear. These Mae Wests are really ingenious. They are yellow. Once you are in the sea you pull a tag which releases a colourful dye which is readily sighted by searching aircraft.

Because we arrived here on pay day and missed our pay we shall have to wait another fortnight – so I shall be without pay for three weeks. I've managed to get over this by borrowing but please could you send me ten bob, Mother? I will post it back to you on pay day.

The view from outside my hut is wizard – one of the highest points in Scotland. It rather reminds me of the Downs on a larger scale. It is climbable and I had intended to tackle it this afternoon, but it is raining and the summit is clouded over. On a sunny day one can see large stone cairns on the top which have been there a hundred years. The real reason I want to climb it though, is to gather some of the purple heather and send you a sprig. I will try again next week.

Next week also I hope to get to Inverness where reputation has it the best English is spoken.

* The Duke of Kent was killed on active service on 25 August 1942.

I attended a 'brevet' parade yesterday when the fellows who had completed the course were on parade. After the ceremony we marched past the CO to the music of our own drum and bagpipe band. We realised then that we really were in Scotland.

Next week our squad start flying in the coffins (Bothas) as we affectionately term these death-traps. With all our chute harness, flying kit and Mae Wests, feeling like trussed turkeys, we somehow made our way to the kite to carry out our gunnery exercises.

Your affectionate son
Edwin

P.S. Have just discovered that the capital of Switzerland
     is nearer London than Evanton.

Hut 194
T Wing
RAF Evanton
Ross-shire

6th September 1942

My dear Mother,

I have now reached the half-way mark in this course and am having to work very hard to make the required progress. The course is short but intensive.

The weather all this week has been putrid – low clouds, ground mist and rain all the time. No good for flying. On my last trip we had the Group Captain of the station instead of the usual Sgt/Pilot. He does a spot of flying occasionally to keep his hand in. We found him rather better over the intercom than the average Pole with his smattering of English.

Bearing in mind your advice, Mother, not to risk my life for any heather, I enclose some of the pink variety obtained from Tain whilst on the range shooting up a model of an Me 110 (which I seldom hit …)

The food continues to be good, and on the whole the camp is one of the best I have known.

Your affectionate son
Edwin

The intensity of training is indicated by the constant moves from one station to another. They were needed to train all different members of the crew. Edwin's wireless telegraphy and gunnery training plus air experience were vitally important. So too were the duties of the pilot, second pilot and the navigator. All of these had to be trained to a high level of competence and welded into a close-knit crew.

RAF personnel were traversing the country like a vast shifting population.

By now, too, the country had to assimilate into its camps and bases all the necessary facilities for the United States' air fleets, arriving in this country in ever-increasing numbers.

No.2 Sergeants Mess
RAF Station
Harwell
nr Didcot
Berks

24th September 1942

My dear Mother,

I have arrived safely at this huge camp and am settling down in the Sergeants mess. The course lasts twelve weeks and then I should get seven days leave. The food is very good and the ante room is comfortably furnished with easy chairs and a radio. I shan't be flying for about three weeks but the time will be occupied with lectures and more lectures.

I have had the first of what promises to be many 'jabs'. Yellow fever was the first – but it's given me no discomfort.

When I first arrived in the dormitory I pointed to an empty bed and said 'Is this anyone's?' 'No,' came the answer, 'He's missing.'

Your affectionate son
Edwin

No.2 Sergeants Mess
RAF Station
Harwell
nr Didcot
Berks

1st October 1942

My dear Mother,

I have been moved to this little village of East Ilsley. I have comfortable quarters in the Old Rectory building. It is a very old, rambling manor but some of the rooms are quite cosy. To enable us to reach camp – four miles away – we have all been loaned bicycles for the duration of our stay. We now realise what a hilly county this is!

I share a room with two jolly good fellows, one an Irishman and the other English. Last Saturday we three hitch-hiked to Oxford managing to get a lift in a Vauxhall owned by a Spitfire factory manager.

We went to a local hop which was crowded with servicemen: the band consisted of a woman pianist, a woman accordionist and a young fellow of 60-odd beating out the rhythm on the drums. It was a strange combination with a limited repertoire: it played <u>Lovely Weekend</u> four times.

Last night I flew in the front turret of a Wimpey and after loading the guns in the air (no mean feat) I fired off a thousand rounds at a drogue flying 600ft above us. Good fun!

Your affectionate son
Edwin

No.2 Sergeants Mess
RAF Station
Harwell
nr Didcot
Berks

6th October 1942

My dear Mother,

I met an old friend from Cambridge who has been here for months – having been grounded. He and I shared a room and it is very interesting to hear news of the boys I knew – most of whom appear to have gone for a burton.

My two friends and I spent a happy time in Oxford on Sunday. The place is crowded out with Johnnie Doughboys. I got into conversation with one fellow who had three stripes upside down. He told me his ambition was to join the RAF. I told him I could think of better things. He said he came from Dixieland and his friend came from Tennessee. When I left him he was trying to open a <u>pound tin</u> of salted peanuts with a fork. However, I enjoyed the Chesterfields he handed round.

Your affectionate son
Edwin

P.S. Do you know the lyrics of <u>Tangerine</u>,
<u>Skylark</u> and <u>Jealousy</u>?

No.2 Sergeants Mess
RAF Station
Harwell
nr Didcot
Berks

20th October 1942

My dear Mother,

Having arrived back safely after such a pleasant weekend at home my worst fears have been realised. Another fellow and I failed to make the grade and have to take the course again. This is by no means a serious matter – it simply means I'm a bit dimmer than the rest of the class – as regards theoretical matters anyway. It will mean losing my two friends, Freddy and Don, but having been in the service so long one becomes accustomed to short friendships.

Thirty minutes ago I came in looking as if I'd been dragged from a pond. Several of us were caught in a heavy downpour of rain as we cycled to the Rectory in record time. We've all washed and changed our clothing. I don't know why but it seems to have cheered us up.

If you forward grandmother's Brazilian address I will try and dash off a few lines. Should I commence 'My dear Grandmother' and end 'Your affectionate grandson'?

Your affectionate son

Edwin

No.2 Sergeants Mess
RAF Station
Harwell
nr Didcot
Berks

1st November 1942

My dear Mother,

I am writing this letter at 11am in the YM building at Oxford having just had breakfast. I was not lucky enough to get a weekend pass so caught a train to Oxford. Despite the drenching rain outside there is a pleasant atmosphere in here. Johnny is reading an article headed <u>Great Issues at Stake in the Middle East</u>: there are four other airmen here and a number of Yanks in their various uniforms. An A/C plonk is banging away at the piano with the Americans looking bewildered as we join in the choruses.

I was talking to one of the Americans earlier. He was impressed by the atmosphere of war over here when he arrived. He remarked 'The folks back home don't realise what it's like in England what with the rationing and restricted transport.'

I was also talking to a pilot from a nearby 'drome who is awaiting a court martial. His crime was flying a Whitley over Oxford towing a glider at 50 feet! His excuse was that he was feeling cheesed at the time.

We were issued with more kit today. I received a fur-lined Irving leather jacket: it has a hood in case of ditching. It is coloured yellow for ease of identification from the air. I was also issued with three pairs of long pants and three vests. So there may be some truth in the rumour that we'll be sent to the Middle East!

As you know, my best uniform is fit only for a dustman, so I decided to do something about it. I ambled along to the tailor shop and managed to get my uniform condemned – after some useful work with a razor blade. I then had to obtain a chit signed by the adjutant. So far so good. But at the stores things weren't going so well. So I spun the old yarn that I was getting married in a few days and consequently had to look smart. (One has to stoop to the lowest things to get what you want.) When I had said this, things changed very quickly. A Waaf said she would take responsibility in the absence of the Flight Lieutenant and issued me with a new tunic and then brought three pairs of trousers to choose from to ensure a good match. I left the stores five minutes later with the good wishes from all!

Your affectionate son
Edwin

Sergeants Mess
RAF Station
Hampstead Norris
nr Newbury
Berks

9th November 1942

My dear Mother,

The above address will tell you I was successful in my last exam and was posted here last Wednesday.

Our job here is to crew up with a navigator and do several day and night cross country trips. I have already made two three-hour trips, including one yesterday to York and back. My navigator (my junior by a year) was at ITW at Cambridge and lives at Ilford. The object is to learn to work as a team and eventually go on ops together.

I've received a letter from Molly to say that Malcolm is a prisoner of war in Germany: he and the front gunner were the only survivors when they crashed. Molly says that several of his friends have been turning up in the POW camp.

It's great news from the Middle East, isn't it?

Your affectionate son
Edwin

For three months two army commanders had been facing each other barely 60 miles from Cairo. The commander of the Axis forces was General Rommel (the Desert Fox), master of the mobile battle; against him was General Bernard Montgomery, master of the set-piece battle and ruthlessly professional in his soldiering. Each commander had at his call dense concentrations of weaponry.

On the night of 23/24 October a tremendous artillery bombardment opened along a 6-mile front at El Alamein.

Montgomery's offensive routed the German Afrika Korps, captured tens of thousands of Italians and the advance became a pursuit. It was not to finish until the end of January 1943 with the capture of Tripoli.

Sergeants Mess
RAF Station
Hampstead Norris
nr Newbury
Berks

19th November 1942

My dear Mother

I heard the Victory Bells last Sunday in the old historic city of Bath.*

Last Saturday we were up on a three hour cross country trip in putrid weather. When we arrived back at base we were diverted to one of our satelites at Bath where the sun was still shining. There were two more of our Ansons there. We were all given a meal in their wizard mess and told we were to stay the night.

We decided to visit Bath for the evening, so all twelve of us hitch-hiked into town wearing our battledress and flying boots. Much to our amazement we were not spotted by any SPs. Later in the evening we went to a dance in the Pavilion – having to dance with flying boots on.

Almost the same thing happened on Tuesday on a flight to the west coast of Scotland. We ended up at a hotel in Ayr (Robert Burns' home-town). I'm considering wearing my best blues for the next flight!

I now have only two more trips to do – both night ones. In a week or two I shall be getting a week's leave – and shall then start on Wimpeys.

Your affectionate son
Edwin

* The Eighth Army breakout from the El Alamein entrenchment started on 22 October and its advance continued for weeks. The victory was celebrated by the ringing of church bells, silenced since 1940.

Sergeants Mess
RAF Station
Harwell
nr Didcot
Berks

10th December 1942

My dear Mother,

Enclosed with the ration money is a chit for half a dozen handker-chieves – all that we are allowed officially. Pyjamas are not approved: I was told we are not expected to sleep in pyjamas.

I haven't had the luck to be flighted yet and am filling in time with guns and wireless – stuff we did months ago.

We have had three prangs during the past week – writing off both air-craft and crews.

'Canada' has just gone on leave and has left a pound tin of pure Canadian butter for Nobby and me to dispose of. It is delicious!

Thank you again for the best leave ever.

Your affectionate son
Edwin

Sergeants Mess
RAF Station
Harwell
nr Didcot
Berks

18th December 1942

My dear Mother,

Sorry I forgot to enclose the clothing coupons: here they are.

Luckily I have been formed into a complete crew, all of whom come from London. We should have gone up today for the first time but the weather was foul and we were grounded. You may remember my talking about my old friend Wee Baxter from Blackpool. He was killed in a night crash last Tuesday, poor old chap. Only last week we were talking about prangs and he said 'I shall be all right, I have a good pilot.' They say that only the good die young …

Your affectionate son
Edwin

ROYAL AIR FORCE
HARWELL

Best Wishes
for
Christmas and the New Year

To Mother, Pop, Margaret & David – from Edwin

Sergeants Mess
RAF Station
Harwell
nr Didcot
Berks

27th December 1942

My dear Mother,

I was out of bed at 10 o'clock on Xmas Day and strolled along to the Smoking Room to find a brass band blaring away and everyone drinking pints of beer. By the time the meal was ready everyone was feeling pretty merry. We had a very good meal with turkey and plum duff. Later there was a cinema show and a dance.

Yesterday – Boxing Day – was a full working day, but the weather kept us grounded. So far our crew have only made one flight together. We now have a 'Bomb Slinger' named Dickson whom we call Dixie. When we aren't flying – and that is often because of our old friends Ground Mist and Ground Haze – we spend our time in the crew room with nothing to do except read and write.

Will you please enclose the prisoner of war form with your next letter so I can write to Malcolm.

Your affectionate son
Edwin

Sergeants Mess
RAF Station
Harwell
nr Didcot
Berks

10th January 1943

My dear Mother,

Have I told you of the good rations we are issued with when we go flying? An orange, chewing gum, sweets, ham or cheese sandwiches. Sometimes I think it worthwhile flying even in this freezing weather in order to get these rations.

So far we have worked very well as a crew. While flying over the Irish Sea on the way to Douglas the other day the skipper invited me up front to do a bit of dual flying – and offered me a cigarette at the same time. The only advantage of Yankee kites is that they are supplied with ash-trays!

We are due to fly again tonight and after an early tea at 3.30 shall go for the briefing – but the weather is clamping down.

A Waaf officer introduced me to an Intelligence officer from the Argentine who knew David Joyce very well. He told me that David had almost completed his tour of ops before he was shot down and killed. A friend from the Argentine wrote to him and mentioned how very cut up Uncle Dudley was about the whole affair.

I enclose a piece of peel to prove that there are such things as oranges in the country.

Your affectionate son
Edwin

Sergeants Mess
RAF Station
Harwell
nr Didcot
Berks

22nd January 1943

My dear Mother,

We only have two more night trips and then we shall be posted – and sent on leave. We've been waiting a week to get these trips in. Last night we set off but were recalled because the weather started closing in. We got as far as the north of England but as we only completed 3 hours flying we didn't qualify for ham and eggs on our return which specially disappointed our rear gunner, Pat, who goes a bundle on bacon, ham and eggs. He was trained in South Africa: I am the only one of our crew who was trained in England.

I have been saving up bags of sweets for you and Pegs so you may use up all your coupons. I'm afraid chocolate is too much of a temptation for me.

Flying has been cancelled for tonight so I shall go to the camp cinema to see <u>Hatters Castle</u>.

Your affectionate son
Edwin

No. 6 Course
4 Group Battle School
RAF Driffield
East Yorkshire

19th February 1943

My dear Mother,

I arrived here safely for the toughening up course. It's to be one of those commando affairs with swimming rivers in full kit (not flying kit surely!) The course will include two night manoeuvres one of which will consist of being taken twenty miles from camp and with no money nor identity card, to dodge the police and Home Guard who will be looking for us; and to return to camp in nine hours. It should be exciting.

We have made a start on the rifle drill. We now have to do a cross country run which will probably be the end of all of us! We hear that we won't be doing any flying here but will be posted to a conversion course next Monday.

Your affectionate son
Edwin

Sergeants Mess
RAF Marston Moor
nr Wetherby
Yorkshire

26th February 1943

My dear Mother,

Marston Moor is ten miles from York. The camp is one of the dispersal types, all modern inconveniences with bags of walking to and from our quarters.

This is the course where we fly in Halifaxes, pick up another air gunner and a flight engineer. After two or three weeks we'll be posted to a squadron.

At Driffield we underwent our intensive training – and I enjoyed the experience. The Army Assault Course consisted of smoke screens, bullets and noises, scaling a 10ft wall, climbing along a wire stretched between two trees, crossing a river by walking gingerly on fallen logs – all at the double with a rifle! I take my hat off to every infantryman after this gruelling course.

Our skipper has managed to bag a flight engineer so all we await now is an extra gunner for the mid-upper turret.

Hoping to see you all soon, but the chances of seeing David before he goes off to the Navy next month are rather remote.

Your affectionate son
Edwin

P.S. The railway station for this camp is Cattell:
an ironically appropriate name considering
the travelling conditions!

Edwin did not manage to see David again before he left to join the training establishment HMS *Collingwood*. Within weeks mother had to endure the anxiety of having one son on operations with Bomber Command and the other at sea in an escort vessel. It was a heavy burden to bear.

Sergeants Mess
RAF Marston Moor
nr Wetherby
Yorkshire

1st March 1943

My dear Mother,

Although we only arrived here on Friday I spent an enjoyable time in York on Saturday with Dixie, Pat and Ted. We had a splendid lunch after which Ted and Pat saw the film <u>In Which We Serve</u> while Dixie and I visited York Minster: he spoke quite knowledgeably about it. We enjoyed tea among numerous Fleet Air Arm pilots and commanders – and gorged ourselves. In the evening we visited Betty's Bar which was crowded with air crew. It is said that if you want to know where the RAF are operating any night you need only pop in there.

Bill is going solo on a Halifax tomorrow so he can be 2nd pilot in our crew. Incidentally, the wireless operator has just about the most comfortable seat in the kite, just below the pilot and nearest the escape hatch! Four pilots went on ops the other night as 2nd pilots to gain experience. They all say it was a piece of cake.

Your affectionate son
Edwin

Bomber Command's nightly offensive with about 250 aircraft was failing to achieve the success hoped for. It was resolved to unleash a thousand bomber raid and Cologne was selected for this spectacular event. In fact 1,046 aircraft were planned to attack. In the event 910 reached the target and 39 aircraft were lost. 13,000 homes were wrecked and there were 5,000 casualties, including 469 killed. Yet despite the damage and the casualties Cologne survived. But the mass raid impressed friend and foe that the initiative lay with the Allies. The RAF was to continue its night raids while the USAAF would employ its Flying Fortresses and Liberator bombers in daylight operations. The losses on both sides were horrendous: Hamburg was devastated and Berlin pounded to destruction.

As the tide of victory swept across Europe the Germans suffered dearly while the attacks on London diminished.

More importantly the Battle of the Atlantic was won in May 1943 with the sinking of forty-one U-boats in the one month.

Sergeants Mess
RAF Marston Moor
nr Wetherby
Yorkshire

15th March 1943

My dear Mother,

You are quite correct, we shan't go on ops until we are posted to a squadron. I have done about twenty hours flying here including two cross country runs, the last covering about 900 miles in 5 hours. I enjoyed the sensation enormously. We were to do another flight tonight, but 'the ceiling was on the deck' so flying was scrubbed at 8 o'clock. I was back in the mess in time to hear excerpts from Dancing Years on the radio.

I was talking to a tail-end Charlie [a rear gunner] on Sunday and he said Essen had another fearful bashing. I think it must be pretty grim over there. We've had a few alerts here but no bombs have been dropped within miles. It worries me when I read that Jerry has been busy over London.

Your affectionate son
Edwin

Sergeants Mess
RAF Marston Moor
nr Wetherby
Yorkshire

24th March 1943

My dear Mother,

I thought of you and David on the 22nd and trust that he arrived at his depot safely.

With a spot of luck we should finish in a day or two and then get posted. When we do finish, Mother, we stand a chance of getting a 48 hour pass and although we shall not get a railway warrant I should love to come home and see you all before my posting to a squadron. The return fare is twenty-eight shillings, so Mother, please draw on my 'savings' so I can have a pleasant time before a squadron. I am sure you will understand: leave will not be any too frequent in the future, so do not be surprised to see me in the next five days.

We had a spot of excitement last Friday when our kite crashed on take off but none of us was hurt. And the MO was on the spot: he was flying us because he likes the experience. We were taking off with a cross wind which swung us round to port, during which we lost our undercart, broke all the props and ripped the engines to shreds. The flight engineer, Ron, had the presence of mind to turn off all the fuel cocks to prevent fires.

They say you aren't an airman until you've had a prang or two ...

Your affectionate son
Edwin

The following letter from Edwin's mother failed to reach him. It was returned to sender marked 'Not Known' although it was correctly addressed.

38 Highstone Avenue
Wanstead
London E11

31st March 1943

My dear Edwin,

I received your letter dated 24th March last Friday, 26th, in which you said you would probably get 48 hours and be home within 5 days. When I read your letter I thought you would expect me to have drawn the money for you by the time you got home, which I did, but when you didn't arrive home by Sunday, it suddenly occurred to me that you might have wanted it for your fare and I should have sent it to you. As you didn't arrive on Monday, Daddy sent you a reply paid telegram yesterday morning, Tuesday 30th, asking if you wanted us to send your fare. Up till now (Wed. 8pm) we haven't even got an answer to that. What really happened, Edwin. Posted without leave, or haven't you been able to get your last bit of flying in yet? Of course, we would all love to see you, and certainly come home if you only get twelve hours so long as you manage it. Perhaps you are already posted nearer home? I do hope to see you or hear from you soon.

My son, I hope everything is well with you. Don't think I let you down, will you? I could have and would have sent your fare immediately if I had understood that was what you wanted me to do. God bless you and keep you safe, my son.

With love
Mother

Sergeants Mess
RAF Station
Linton-on-Ouse
nr York

2nd April 1943

My dear Mother

I am so sorry I haven't written earlier but I have been posted to this squadron and have been rather busy.

The weather has been very poor for the past few days although the howling wind has dropped today. Consequently, our crew are to do our first op tonight. Do not worry yourself because this squadron has a fine reputation and loses few kites. We have been waiting the last few days for this job and all feel very bucked and excited. (Note the steady hand.) There are many things I'd like to mention but dare not in case the letter is read by the censor. We were briefed about an hour ago.

We were very surprised and not a little angry not to get a 48 hour pass from Marston Moor, but apparently our services were required by this squadron and we were posted here direct.

If you will forward Aunt Emily and Florence's address in São Paulo I shall write to them. But please PRINT the addresses, Mother, and supply information about air mail stamps.

I am writing this while waiting for our night flying supper which I hope will include an egg!

Everyone appears to be shoving off for the meal so I think I will join the merry boys. Keep your fingers crossed!

Your affectionate son
Edwin

Operations Record Book: 78 Squadron

2.4.43 Halifax II DT 768

> Up 1922
> Down 0133

Target was attacked and bombed at 22.23 hours from a height of 14,000ft. Identified by T. I. red and green markers and also visually by the river. Red markers were in the bomb-sight when bombs were released and own bombs seen to burst near stern red marker. Aircraft arrived early over the target and fires had been set alight but after leaving the target area two fires were seen. One was much larger than the other and the glow of the flames could be seen when leaving the north French coast. Successful photos were taken showing smoke screen and T. I. Markers. No cloud. Slight haze over target area.

Sergeants Mess
RAF Station
Linton-on-Ouse
nr York

8th April 1943

My dear Mother,

I received Peggy's letter yesterday much to my delight. I thought you had forgotten me!

You are right in guessing St Nazaire as our target. We gave it something to remember us by last Thursday night and we returned without so much as a scratch on K for Kathleen. The whole business was little different from an ordinary cross country night flight. But what gave us all a thrill was when we crossed the French coast and knew we were well on the way to our target. Actually we arrived there nine minutes ahead of the bombing time so we had to circle it until we could bomb. The flak was said to have been light by the veterans but there was sufficient to keep us weaving and turning. A searchlight swept across us but passed on … much to our joy. We saw another unfortunate kite coned by searchlights and what seemed like all the guns in creation having a crack at him.

We haven't done any more operations yet: the weather has been very windy and cold and we have had an awful stroke of bad luck.

On Friday's raid on Essen we lost our navigator, Ted. He substituted for another navigator who was sick and could not fly. Of course, we don't know what happened. He has simply been posted missing. He lived with his widowed mother in Ilford and had no brothers or sisters.

Our pilot, Bill, acted as 2nd Pilot on the raid to Kiel on Saturday night and we were all glad to see him back on Sunday morning. Every pilot has to do two trips to Germany as 2nd pilot for the experience. The op to St Nazaire is regarded as an ordinary cross country by our Flight Commander!

This is all very cheerless news to write home, but although Ted is missing we shall soon get another navigator and we hope sincerely that he knows his onions, because we don't want to fool around with too many cross country trips just for his experience.

As regards leave, Mother, I should get twelve days in about four or five weeks time. This will suit our purposes admirably because Pat, the rear gunner, will be twenty-one in May and is going to have a GRAND PARTY.

I have never in all my two-and-a-half years in the RAF had so much time to spare. I inspect the wireless equipment of our kite in the morning and sign as having done so and if no ops, I buzz off to York in the afternoon with the crew.

Due to a heck of a lot of dancing both shoes are in need of repair and I cannot have them repaired in York. Will you please send me an old pair? And send them as soon, soon, soon as you can. I don't want to be deprived of my favourite enjoyment. I will reward your kindness by saving some more sweets and a tin of orange juice.

I shan't bother you anymore with shirts and collars to wash because I have found a reliable laundry in York called Jock Ching! Try to imagine the Chinese owner talking with a broad Yorkshire accent!

We have been searching for ideas for a name for our kite. Most names fellows have chosen for their kites are indelicate. Much to my crew's pleasure I hit upon the idea of 'Happy Go Lucky'. The decision was unanimous.

Love and kisses to all

Your affectionate son
Edwin

P.S. Please don't forget the shoes, Mother.

Part Three

MISSING IN ACTION AND THE AFTERMATH

1943–61

17TH APRIL 1943

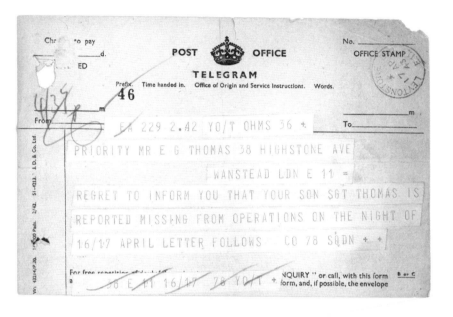

Operations Record Book: 78 Squadron

Operations Order No 491: 16.4.43

Total 269 aircraft:	16 PFF
	92 Stirlings of 3 Group
	12 Halifaxes of 4 Group
	149 Wellingtons of 1, 4 and 6 Groups

3 Aircraft of 78 Squadron

First aircraft take off 21.15

Colne Point	22.29
Dungeness	22.49
On Target	00.47
Off Target	00.57
St Valery en Caux	02.37
Abingdon	03.24
Base	04.22

13 aircraft detailed for operations. 10 aircraft took off to attack the Skoda works at Pilsen. 8 reached and attacked the target area with varying results and the two remaining aircraft were reported missing. The remaining three aircraft took off to attack Mannheim. 1 aircraft is missing from this operation. 1 aircraft reached and attacked the target area whilst the third aircraft abandoned its mission owing to being damaged by flak after being coned by searchlights. 16.4.43 Halifax 2. No JB 780 1316 508

Off 21.15 Nothing heard from this aircraft since take off. Presume missing.

No. 78 Squadron,
Royal Air Force,
Linton on Ouse,
Yorks.

18th April 1943.

Dear Mr. Thomas,

It is with the deepest feelings of sorrow that I have
to confirm my telegram telling you that your son, Sgt. Thomas,
failed to return from the raid on Mannheim on the night of
16/17th April. I am afraid that there is absolutely no inform=
ation that we can give you as no signal was received after the
aircraft took off, and none of the crews operating that night
had anything to report.

It is quite possible of course that he and the other
members of the crew landed safely on enemy territory and are now
safe, but prisoners of war, which we sincerely hope is the case,
but nothing definite is known at the moment. You may be assured
that I will let you know at once should any news come through.
If you hear anything before we do as sometimes happens, we
should be very grateful if you would let us know immediately.

Your son's going has left a sad gap, not only in the
work of the Squadron, where his enthusiam for his work made him
one of our promising Wireless Operators, although he had only
been with us for a short while, but also in the Sergeants Mess,
where he had found many good friends. We all realise that
nothing we can say can do anything to relieve the grief and
anxiety this news must cause you, but we should like you to know
that we share these feelings. I trust that you will accept this
letter as a sincere expression of the sympathy we all feel for
you in your loss.

If there is anything I can do to help I trust that
you will let me know without hesitation. I feel that you might
like to know the names of those who were with your son on the
night in question, and I enclose a list giving their names and
next of kin.

Yours sincerely
G.B. Warner.

Wing Commander, Commanding,
No. 78 Squadron, R.A.F.

Mr. E.G. Thomas,
38, Highstone Avenue,
Wanstead, Essex.

1387760 Sgt Illingworth, W.		= Pilot
Next of Kin: Wife	Name:	Mrs L. D. Illingworth 47 Chauntler Road Custom House London E16
1316504 Sgt West, C.G.		= Navigator
Next of Kin: Father	Name:	Mr W. A. West 15 Heol Tirdu Cwn Rhydyceirw Morriston, Swansea
125643 P/O H. D. Dixon		= Bombardier
Next of Kin: Father	Name:	Rev H. H. Dixon 26 Alleyn Road W. Dulwich, London SE21
1270671 Sgt Thomas, E. G.		= Wireless Operator
Next of Kin: Father	Name:	Mr E. G. Thomas 38 Highstone Avenue Wanstead, Essex
995589 Sgt Woodhall, R.		= Flight Engineer
Next of Kin: Mother	Name:	Mrs R. Woodhall Full Sutton, Yorks
1384483 Sgt Patton, S. W.		= Air Gunner
Next of Kin: Mother	Name:	Mrs A. M. Patton 128 Farmers Road London, SE5
1652776 Sgt Watkins, D.E.		= Air Gunner
Next of Kin: Father	Name:	Mr A. W. Watkins 27 Waterloo Place Brynmill, Swansea

Telephone No. : SPRINGWELL (GLOUCESTER) 2204
Telegraphic Address :
RECORDS TELEX, GLOUCESTER.
Any communications on the
subject of this letter should
be addressed to :—
AIR OFFICER i/c RECORDS,
    Address as opposite,
and the following number
quoted :—

Your Ref. : ...C7/..1270671

RECORD OFFICE,

ROYAL AIR FORCE,

GLOUCESTER.

Date....19th April 1943

Dear Sir,

    I regret to confirm that your son No.
1270671 Sergeant Edwin Gordon THOMAS, of No. 78
Squadron, Royal Air Force, is missing, the aircraft
of which he was the wireless operator and air gunner
having failed to return to its base on the night of
the 16th/17th April 1943 from an operational flight.

    This does not necessarily mean that he
is killed or wounded. I will communicate with you
again immediately I have any further news and would
be obliged if you, on your part, would write to me
should you hear anything of your son from unofficial
sources.

    May I assure you of the sympathy of the
Royal Air Force with you in your anxiety.

        I am,
           Dear Sir,
             Your obedient Servant,

            Air Commodore,
            Air Officer i/c Records,
            ROYAL   AIR   FORCE.

F.G. Thomas Esq.,
38 High Stone Avenue,
WANSTEAD,
Essex.

CONFIDENTIAL NOTICE

The names of all who lose their lives or are wounded or reported missing while serving with the Royal Air Force will appear in the official casualty lists published from time to time in the Press.

Any publication of the date, place or circumstances of a casualty, and particularly any reference to the unit concerned, might give valuable information to the enemy, and for this reason, only the name, rank and Service number are included in the official lists.

Relatives are particularly requested, in the national interest, to ensure that any notices published privately do not disclose the date, place or circumstances of the casualty or the unit.

The Press have been asked to co-operate in ensuring that no information of value to the enemy is published.

Notes for the General Information and Guidance of the Next-of-Kin or other Relatives of Airmen reported Missing, Deceased, Prisoners of War or Interned. (Where the words 'Airman' or 'Airmen' appear they are to be construed as including 'Airwoman' and 'Airwomen'.)

PART I AIRMEN REPORTED MISSING

1. Private Effects under RAF Control

(i) The private effects under RAF control of an airman reported missing whilst serving with a unit in the United Kingdom, in Iceland, or in Gibraltar are forwarded to the Central Depository, Colnbrook, near Slough [...] for retention in safe custody. This does not apply to bulky items such as motor cars, or large wireless sets. These are retained in safe custody by the station. Any cash found among the effects is handed over to the Accountant Officer [...]

(iii) The private effects of airmen reported missing cannot normally be released unless and until death is officially presumed to have occurred, which will be done whenever absolutely conclusive evidence of death is received [...] When evidence of death is not received within six months of the date on which the airman was reported missing, action will be taken by the Air Ministry to presume death for official purposes [...]

(iv) After death has been officially presumed the effects will be released on the instructions of the Air Ministry (Accounts 13), Whittington Road, Worcester, subject to it having been ascertained who is the person legally entitled to receive them.

(v) The foregoing only applies to the effects under RAF control. It will be appreciated that the RAF cannot accept responsibility for articles left outside camp or quarters e.g. at the houses of friends.

2. Family and Dependents' Allowances and Pay

(i) Family and Dependents' allowances (together with qualifying and voluntary allotments) and voluntary allotments to persons within certain degrees of relationship, if in payment before the airman is reported missing, will continue to be paid, and pay credited to the airman's account, for four weeks after the date of notification of the casualty, or until death is established or presumed, whichever is the earlier. In other cases, pay ceases when an airman is missing.

As soon as the news of Edwin's loss became known the letters of condolences started arriving. Aunt Lydia wrote touchingly of hearing the RAF bombers going over the Sussex coast almost nightly. She and Aunt Ethel (both father's sisters) comforted mother. Among all the official letters there were letters from neighbours, from David's scout master, Mr Day, from mother's sister Emily there came a cable. Kitty Bayford, and many other friends and neighbours wrote – including Lilian Illingworth, wife of one of Edwin's crew members.

NLT TELEGRAM FROM SÃO PAULO BRAZIL 21ST APRIL 1943 TO NELLIE THOMAS 38 HIGHSTONE AVENUE CAMBRIDGE PARK WANSTEAD = TERRIBLY UPSET SAD NEWS RECEIVED TODAY. FAMILY WITH YOU IN THOUGHT. ANXIOUSLY HOPING BEST = EMILY BARBOSA +

Tuffcleys
Burgess Hill
Sussex

21st April 1943

My dear Edwin,

I cannot tell you how sorry we are to hear the bad news of Edwin and most earnestly hope he may have been able to bale out and be picked up safe later on. It must be a terrible blow to Helen, for Ethel has told me how devoted the boys were to their mother, and how they have never given her the slightest anxiety or worry. It is some consolation to know that Edwin was so very keen on the Air Force and would not have wished to be in any other Service. The RAF are marvellous boys and to hear them going over night after night makes one's heart ache. Give my love to everyone and I do hope you will have some good tidings in the course of the next week or so.

Yours affectionately
Lydia

THE ROYAL AIR FORCE BENEVOLENT FUND

Eaton House

14 Eaton Road

Hove

Sussex

21st April 1943

Dear Mr Thomas,

The Council of the Royal Air Force Benevolent Fund have learnt with much regret that your son is missing, and I am asked to convey to you their very sincere sympathy.

I am to inform you that if your missing son was making a voluntary allotment through official channels while in the Service, you should be receiving a temporary allowance at the moment from the Air Ministry which will continue for a period of 26 weeks pending further information concerning your son.

If the allowance is not being received, you should communicate immediately with the Secretary, Air Ministry, (Accts 7) Dept OA, Redhill, Worcester.

If, however, your missing son was contributing privately to your support, you should make application for the temporary allowance to the Air Ministry as above, forwarding at the same time proof of such assistance.

Should you be in need of some temporary assistance either now or in the future, please let me know and I will arrange for our Representative to interview you at the earliest opportunity.

In the meantime, if I can help or advise in any way perhaps you will kindly write to me, otherwise please do not trouble to answer this letter.

Yours truly,

Squadron Leader

Joint Secretary

Carskiey
Southend
Argyllshire

23 April 1943

My dear Helen and Edwin,

I am distressed to hear your bad news and feel so sorry for you all in your great sorrow. But you must not give up hope: Edwin is reported missing. He may be a prisoner of war. I know it is a great strain on one not knowing: but you have the consolation of knowing he was brave and gave himself for his King and Country to fight for you and mankind. There could be no nobler death. This war is not an ordinary war, but a crusade …

You too can be brave by consoling yourself that he did the right thing and your memories will always be bright and you will be a proud mother.

I shall always think of him as alive: I cannot think of any of our boys who have gone in this war as dead – I feel they are coming back all the time.

Do be brave for Edwin's sake. I feel I have not expressed myself very well but you have my heartfelt sympathy.

Yours affectionately
Ethel

62 Canterbury Avenue
Ilford
Essex

Dear Mrs Thomas,

I just called to see you for a few minutes.

I hope that you are well.

Best wishes and love
Jessie Jones

43 Bulwer Court
Leytonstone
London E I I

27th April 1943

Dear Mrs Thomas,

I was deeply grieved to hear the sad news about Edwin. There's so very little one can say or do in the circumstances and it is simply a case of waiting and hoping for better news …

Yours sincerely
R. B. Day

44 Highstone Avenue
Wanstead
London E I I

Sunday

Dear Mr & Mrs Thomas,

It is with deep sorrow we heard about the telegram.

Mr Denny and I would like you to accept our deepest sympathy at such time.

Yours very sincerely
Hilda Denny

Reference LIN.908/78S/126/P.1

RAF Station
Linton-on-Ouse
York

2nd May 1943

Dear Mr Thomas,

I am writing to inform you that the personal effects of your son, Sergeant E. Thomas, have now been forwarded to:

The President, Standing Committee of Adjustment,
RAF Central Depository
Colnbrook, Slough, Bucks.

Any information you desire regarding these effects should now be obtained from the President, who will in any case be writing to you at an early date.

A Post Office Savings Bank Book – Maidstone 63464 – found amongst the effects was extracted and has been forwarded to the Air Ministry for necessary action: and a sum of £3/0/od in cash has been handed to the Accountant Officer to be credited to your son's non-effective account.

Please accept my deepest sympathy with you during this anxious time of waiting, and if there is anything I can do to help, please do not hesitate to let me know.

Yours sincerely
F. Cobb W/O
for Group Captain
Commanding RAF Station
Linton-on-Ouse York

Oxford

14th May 1943

Dear Eddie

I feel almost ashamed to put the date on the paper – 14th May – and your letter was dated 11th February: dear me, how scandalous.

To begin with, I received your letter while in bed suffering a bad attack of flu. Well, after careful recovery, the work at the office had attained such terrific heights it took March and April to get things back more or less to normal … I feel frightfully guilty about all this, especially after you took the trouble to write to me.

Are you still up in the wilds of Yorkshire on Halifaxes? I suppose this is very old news now and what's the betting you have to look first at the signature of this letter and then wrack your brains to think who on earth Valerie is?

I'm sending this attempt of a letter to your home in the hope that your parents will forward it on to you.

Take care of yourself and make an effort to try and be good.

Anyway, lots of luck, and my very best wishes for all time.

Just – Valerie

5 Perry Cottages
Barley Lane
Goodmayes
Essex

17th May 1943

Dear Mrs Thomas,

I do hope that you have received some good news by now; if not, do not give up hope. I feel sure your boy is safe. I pray for him and you at all times, so dear Mrs Thomas, do keep your chin up ...

I am back home now. It is only a little place, but everyone is welcome so if you care to come over and have a talk – it does sometimes do good – please do.

Yours very sincerely
Helen M. Lacey

'Hayburn'
79 St Johns Road
Huddersfield
Yorks

25th May 1943

Dear Friends,

I am staying with Bill's Mum and Dad but I shall be coming back to London on Sunday. I really wish I could stay here for about a month, but work comes first. So I am sorry I have not been to see you, but after such an upset over Bill and the raids I felt that I had better have my holiday early and have a good rest.

You will remember that Bill lent his navigator, Ted, to another crew and he didn't return from a raid. Last week I received a letter from Ted's mother saying that he was safe and a prisoner of war in Germany. She heard the news in just five weeks, so please God we will be hearing some good news now.

Your sincere friend
Lilian (Illingworth)

Oxford

25th May 1943

Dear Mrs Thomas,

Thank you so very much for your letter telling me about Eddie. Words at such a time are so inadequate to express one's feelings and I'm afraid that eloquence has never been one of my assets. But I would like you to know that I feel very, very sad about it all, although I shall not give up hope that one day you will receive the good news that Eddie and the rest of the crew are safe and well. And perhaps when you do hear you will be kind enough to let me know.

I have very pleasant memories of the short time that Eddie was stationed near Oxford, where he and his friends were able to come into the canteen where I help. He was so full of the joys of life and was so very popular with everyone …

Always will I hope and pray that soon you will hear good news of him.

Yours very sincerely

Valerie

27th May 1943

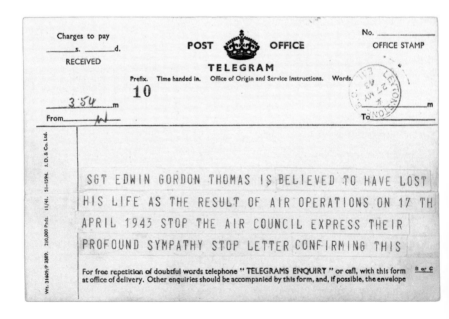

Charges to pay					No.

POST OFFICE

TELEGRAM

Prefix.   Time handed in.   Office of Origin and Service Instructions.   Words.

RECEIVED   OFFICE STAMP

11

3.54 m

From _____

To _____

TELEGRAM FOLLOWS STOP UNDER SECRETARY OF STATE
STOP = 271257 B +

38 P 5920 ONE 27/5/43 1270671 17 1943 271257 B

38 + petition of doubtful words telephone " TELEGRAMS ENQUIRY " or call, with this form
delivery. Other enquiries should be accompanied by this form, and, if possible, the envelope

40 Highstone Avenue
Wanstead
London E11

27th May 1943

My dear Mr & Mrs Thomas,

I have just heard the sad news and I cannot sufficiently express how deeply grieved I feel for you both and for little Peggy and David and all who were near and dear to your dear Edwin.

I felt and hope he would be spared to you. It is too heartbreaking to think about, that such a lovely boy should be taken from you all. I hope you will be given strength ... and courage to bear up under the heavy loss.

Very sincerely yours
Kitty S. Bayford

47 Chauntler Road
Custom House
London E16

Sunday

Dear Mr & Mrs Thomas

I should like to thank you for your kind thoughts of wanting to rush over to see me at a time when things were so dark for you – as they were for myself.

I just can't think of words to express my feelings at the moment, but as you say, we must be as brave as possible.

My thoughts are with you all.

Yours very sincerely
Lilian

County High School for Girls
Cranbrook Road
Ilford
Essex

1st June 1943

Dear Mr & Mrs Thomas,

I am very sorry indeed to hear the bad news about your son. You must have gone through terrible hopes and fears before the final blow. I wish I could express my sympathy for you. Margaret will feel it deeply, too. In some ways I think the first great loss one experiences in life is the worst, but young people are more resilient than older ones. The ordinary school routine is probably the best thing for her and you may be sure we will make allowances for her if any have to be made.

Please do not trouble to answer this letter.

Yours sincerely
E.B. Bull (Headmistress)

Gerrard 9234
xxxxxxxxx

P.403032/5/43/P.4.A.2.

Casualty Branch,
xxxxxxxxxxxxxxxx
77, Oxford Street,
xxxxxxxxxxxxxxxx
London. W.1.

5 June, 1943.

Sir,

     I am commanded by the Air Council to inform you that they have with great regret to confirm the telegram in which you were notified that, in view of information now received from the International Red Cross Committee, your son, Sergeant Edwin Gordon Thomas, Royal Air Force, is believed to have lost his life as the result of air operations on 17th April, 1943.

     The Committee's telegram, quoting official German information, states that the seven occupants of the aircraft in which your son was flying were killed on 17th April, 1943. It contains no information regarding the place of their burial nor any other details.

     Although there is unhappily little reason to doubt the accuracy of this report, the casualty will be recorded as "missing believed killed" until confirmed by further evidence, or until, in the absence of such evidence, it becomes necessary owing to lapse of time to presume for official purposes that death has occurred. In the absence of confirmatory evidence death would not be presumed until at least six months from the date when your son was reported missing.

/The

F. G. Thomas Esq,
  38, High Stone Avenue,
    Wanstead,
      Essex.

     The Air Council desire me to express their deep sympathy with you in your grave anxiety.

     I am, Sir,

       Your obedient Servant,

         J A Smith

'Hayburn'
79 St Johns Road
Huddersfield
Yorks

7th June 1943

Dear Mr & Mrs Thomas,

Many thanks for your letter, but we were sorry you had the same sad news as ourselves. It all just doesn't seem possible. But we must bear this sorrow with fortitude and trust our boys will find Peace.

I feel very deeply for my dear daughter-in-law, Lilian, in her great sorrow. They had just started to build a little world of their own as we all do when we marry – and it all seems to have fallen to pieces. I was so pleased she was here with us when the final news came. She is very brave.

Your letter was a great comfort to us and I shall be delighted to meet you both and should you care to come for a holiday we shall be very pleased to see you.

Yours sincerely
Rose Illingworth
(mother of crewman William Illingworth)

Central Depository
Royal Air Force
Colnbrook
Slough
Bucks

7th June 1943

In reply please quote reference CD/1270671/F 26067

Dear Sir,

The personal effects of your son as listed on the attached inventory have now reached this office from the Unit and will be held in safe custody pending the receipt of further evidence which will enable a conclusive classification of the casualty to be made.

A Post Office Savings Bank book has been forwarded direct to the Air Ministry by the unit.

In the case of casualties reported as 'missing' unless definite evidence comes to light in the meantime, authority to release the effects is not normally received from the Air Ministry until at least six months from the date of the casualty, since official action to presume death is rarely taken before the expiration of that period.

In the case of casualties ultimately reported 'Prisoner of War' the Air Ministry will as a general rule only authorise the release of effects on the written request of the officer or airman concerned. In these circumstances, in order to expedite release, any original letter received from a Prisoner of War in this connection should be forwarded to this office for perusal and early return.

In the meantime may I be permitted to express my sympathy with you in this period of anxiety.

Yours faithfully
A.R. Davies
Squadron Leader, Commanding
RAF Central Depository

TELEPHONE: GERRARD 9234

Extn. ....

Any communications on the
subject of this letter should
be addressed to :—

THE
UNDER SECRETARY
OF STATE,

and the following number
quoted :— P.403032/5/43/P.4.B.3.

Your Ref. ....

AIR MINISTRY

(Casualty Branch),

73-77, OXFORD STREET,

W.1

19ᵗʰ August, 1943

Sir,

I am directed to refer to a letter from
this Department dated 4th June, 1943, and
to inform you with regret that a report has
now been received from the International Red
Cross Committee, which states that your son,
Sergeant Edwin Gordon Thomas, Royal Air
Force, was buried on the 19th April, 1943,
in the English World War Cemetery, Roye,
Somme. This place is about 22 miles south-
east of Amiens, France.

His six comrades who lost their lives in
the same operation are buried in the same
cemetery.

In conveying this information, I am to
express the very sincere sympathy of the
Department with you in your great loss.

/Presumption

F.G. Thomas, Esq.
38, High Stone Avenue,
Wanstead,
Essex.

Presumption of death action will
follow in due course.

I am, Sir,
Your obedient Servant,

I. R. Shreeve

for Director of Personal Services

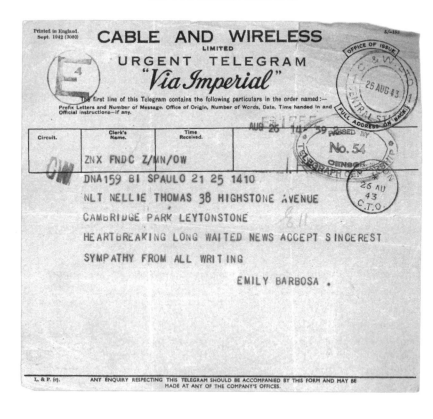

```
Printed in England.
Sept. 1942 (3000)
                CABLE  AND  WIRELESS
                            LIMITED
                 URGENT   TELEGRAM
                  "Via Imperial"
        The first line of this Telegram contains the following particulars in the order named:—
        Prefix Letters and Number of Message, Office of Origin, Number of Words, Date, Time handed in and
        Official Instructions—if any.
```

Circuit.	Clerk's Name.	Time Received.		
	ZNX FNDC Z/MN/OW			No. 54

```
    DNA159 BI SPAULO 21 25 1410

    NLT NELLIE THOMAS 38 HIGHSTONE AVENUE

    CAMBRIDGE PARK LEYTONSTONE

    HEARTBREAKING LONG WAITED NEWS ACCEPT SINCEREST

    SYMPATHY FROM ALL WRITING

                            EMILY BARBOSA .
```

```
L. & P. (c).      ANY ENQUIRY RESPECTING THIS TELEGRAM SHOULD BE ACCOMPANIED BY THIS FORM AND MAY BE
                                 MADE AT ANY OF THE COMPANY'S OFFICES.
```

Caixa Postal 26–B
São Paulo
Brazil

27th August 1943

My dear Nellie,

I realise all too well that no words of mine could possibly bring any comfort to either of you in your great loss no matter how I may try – so I am not going to try other than to express to you my sincerest sympathy and to tell you how during the last four months I have prayed that dear Edwin might somewhere be safe ... my prayers seem to have been in vain. It's all so terribly sad, Nellie dear, and I do wish we were nearer each other so that I might help you in some way.

I don't think I need say you should be proud of the glorious way in which Edwin met his death – because certainly you wouldn't have had him go in any way but fighting for Good Old England and for the cause she is fighting for so splendidly. Nevertheless, it's still a wicked shame that so many of our boys have to lose their lives and be deprived of so much.

I am sending you a clipping from the <u>Gazeta</u> which I am sure you would like to have.

There seems so much I want to say to you, yet am at an utter loss for words in which to express my feelings. My heart goes out to you.

Your affectionate sister, with heaps of love,

Florence

C. H. Dodkin
Caixa Postal 26–B
São Paulo
Brazil

31st August 1943

My dear Nellie,

I should just like to add a line to the letter which Florrie, Emily and Mum have already written, figuratively to give you a squeeze of the hand and to offer my sympathy on the report of Edwin's death. I know that any words from me can mean very little to you, but nevertheless want you to know my thoughts are with you.

Yours sincerely

Dod

GERRARD 9234

TELEPHONE :
    Extn...............

Any communications on the
subject of this letter should
be addressed to :—
        THE
    UNDER SECRETARY
    OF STATE,
and the following number
quoted :—

Your Ref. ....P.403032/43/P.4.B.8.

AIR MINISTRY

(Casualty Branch),

73-77, OXFORD STREET,
W.1.

20 September 1943.

Sir,

   With reference to the letter from
this Department of the 19th August 1943, I am
directed to inform you that action has now been
taken to presume, for official purposes, that
your son, 1270671 Sergeant E.G. Thomas, lost his
life on the 17th April 1943.

   I am to express the sympathy of the
Department with you in your great loss.

     I am, Sir,
      Your obedient Servant,

       D. Bent

   for Director of Personal Services.

F.G. Thomas Esq.,
  38 High Stone Avenue,
    Wanstead,
     ESSEX.

Air Ministry
Whittington Road
Worcester

5th October 1943

Reference: F 857810/43/Accts 13.

Sir,

The Late Sergeant E. G. Thomas

I am directed to acknowledge the receipt of A.M. Form 531 sent to you for completion and to inform you that a further communication will be addressed to you in due course.

I am, Sir,
Your obedient Servant,
N. M. Colley
for Director of Accounts

Air Ministry
Accounts 13
Whittington Road
Worcester

5th October 1943

REGISTERED POST

Dear Sir,

The Late Sergeant E. G. Thomas

I am directed to forward herewith:-
(a) A Post Office Savings Bank Book issued at Maidstone, No. 63464 showing a credit balance of 1sh. od [...]
found among the personal effects, and to inform you that information as to making a claim to the moneys or certificates may be obtained at a Post Office.

I am, Sir,
Your obedient Servant,
W. Taylor
for Director of Accounts

Central Depository
Royal Air Force
Colnbrook
Slough
Bucks

Reference: CD/1270671/F. 26067   7th October 1943

<u>1270671 SGT. THOMAS, E. G.</u>

Dear Sir,

   The Committee of Adjustment composed of myself and two others which is
being held at this office in accordance with Air Ministry instructions to deal with
the estate of the above named, in so far as the Royal Air Force is concerned,
desires to express deep sympathy with you in your bereavement.

   I enclose an inventory of the personal effects held at this office which will be
forwarded to the legal representative of the deceased as soon as Air Ministry
authority for their release is received.

   Monetary matters are not being dealt with at this office but by the Air Ministry
(Accounts 13 Department), Whittingdon Road, Worcester, who will, in due course,
send a statement of the service estate showing all service credits (e.g. cash
found in effects, pay due etc.) and liabilities, and will remit any balance to the
deceased's legal representative. Correspondence relative to these matters, therefore, should not be addressed to this office [...]

Yours faithfully,
A. R. Davies
Squadron Leader Commanding
<u>RAF Central Depository</u>

F.26067

PERSONAL EFFECTS OF 1270671 SGT. THOMAS, E. G.

1 Carton contg:–

3 prs black shoes

1 pr pyjamas

3 toothbrushes

1 wrist watch – damaged

1 envelope containing:
    medallion on chain

1 handkerchief

2 collars

1 pr kid gloves

3 prs socks

2 shirts

2 shaving brushes

1 nail brush

1 cuff link

1 writing case contg:–
    greeting cards, photos,
    envelopes, autograph
    album, 2 diaries

1 wallet

1 bundle letters

1 pr swim trunks

1 pullover

TELEPHONE:
GERRARD 9234
Extn..................

Any communications on the
subject of this letter should
be addressed to :—
THE
UNDER SECRETARY
OF STATE,
and the following number
quoted :— P.403032/43/P4/B7

Your Ref. ....

AIR MINISTRY

(Casualty Branch),

73-77, OXFORD STREET,

W.1.

9 February, 1944.

Sir,

    I am directed to refer to your letter
of the 19th January, 1944, and to forward a
certified notification of the death of your
son, Sergeant E.G. Thomas.

    Such a notification is normally accepted
as proof of death by the Principal Probate
Registry, and will, it is hoped meet the
purpose for which it is required.

        I am, Sir,
           Your obedient Servant,

               m. Crabbe.

        for Director of Personal Services.

E.G. Thomas, Esq.,
    38, Highstone Avenue,
      Wanstead,
        E.11.

P.403032/43/P.4.B.7.

<u>NOTIFICATION OF DEATH.</u>

CERTIFIED that according to the records of this department 1270671 Sergeant Edwin Gordon Thomas, Royal Air Force Volunteer Reserve, was reported missing and is presumed, for official purposes, to have lost his life on the seventeenth day of April 1943 as the result of air operations.

According to a report received from the International Red Cross Committee this airman is buried in the English World War Cemetery, Roye, Somme, France.

for Director of Personal Services.

Dated at
the Air Ministry,
London,
this   9   day of February, 1944.

Air Ministry
Whittington Road
Worcester

14th February 1944

Sir,

<u>The late Sergeant E. G. Thomas</u>

I am directed to inform you that the out turn of your son's service estate is as detailed hereunder:–

Balance of Pay and Allowances	£2. 16. 3.
Service Post War Credit at 6d per day	11. 15. 6.
Cash found in effects	5. 0. 0.
Refund of Income Tax on service emoluments	10. 16. 0.
	£30. 7. 9.

A payable order for this amount in favour of you and your wife is being sent to you under separate cover, and should reach you within the next few days.

I am, Sir,
Your obedient Servant,
W. Taylor
for Director of Accounts

Air Ministry
73–77 Oxford Street
London W1

20th April 1945

Reference: P 403032/4/43/P.4. (B4)

Sir,

I am directed to refer to a letter from this Department dated 19th August 1943, and to inform you that according to a report now received from Paris the number of your son's grave in the British World War Cemetery at Roye, is 14.

I am, Sir,

Your obedient Servant,

Director of Personal Services

Edwin Thomas senior died at the age of fifty-four in July 1945. He had celebrated the end of the war in Europe in May, but in the Far East where his younger son David was serving with the Royal Navy, the Japanese resisted powerfully the advancing Allied forces. His wife, lonelier than ever, sought solace in her daughter, and grieved for the rest of her life.

David came home from the Far East in 1946 having been refused a compassionate early return home. The homecoming when it came was to a depleted family, a now adult sister and marriages to come: grandchildren brought contentment to all except mother whose loss could never be filled.

St Paul's Anglican Church São Paulo

SERVICE OF REMEMBRANCE

and

DEDICATION OF MEMORIAL TABLET

9 November 1947

The Congregation remains standing during the playing

of the

BRAZILIAN NATIONAL ANTHEM

<u>Minister</u>: Dearly beloved, we are met together, in the presence of Almighty God and of the whole company of Heaven, to commemorate and commend to Him [...] those who died that we and our children might live [...]

<u>The Chairman of the British Community Council</u>, addressing the Chaplain, shall say: Reverend Sir, I beseech you, as Chaplain of St Paul's Anglican Church, São Paulo, to receive, dedicate and safeguard this Memorial Tablet, which, in the name of the British Community of São Paulo and District, I now unveil in memory of those of our number who gave their lives in two wars.

<u>The Chaplain</u>: We accept this Tablet in sacred trust and shall guard it reverently in memory of those whose names are thereon recorded [...]

SOUNDING OF 'LAST POST'

TWO MINUTES SILENCE

SOUNDING OF REVEILLE

Then, <u>the President of the British Legion</u> shall say:

> *They shall not grow old, as we that are left grow old.*
> *Age shall not weary them, nor the years condemn.*
> *At the going down of the sun and in the morning*
> *We will remember them.*

Extracts from *The Daily Telegraph* In Memoriam notices:

THOMAS, Edwin Gordon RAFVR killed in action April 16/17 1943.
Lovingly remembered always.

'I have fought the good fight
I have finished the course
I have kept the faith.'

THOMAS, Edwin Gordon, RAFVR, my son, killed in action April 17th 1943.
Deep in my heart you live, beloved and unforgotten – Mother.

THOMAS, Edwin Gordon, RAF. He died a glorious death on April 17 1943
fighting for his country. Remembering today his birthday.

'Softly the leaves of memory fall;
Lovingly I stop to gather them all.'

THE YORK MINSTER THANKSGIVING MEMORIAL
1951

The beautiful shrine which it is proposed to erect in a Chantry in the North Transept of York Minster [...] will be a worthy memorial to the fallen of Nos. 4, 6 and 7 Groups, Bomber Command, Nos. 16 and 18 Groups, Coastal Command and the squadrons of Fighter Command which operated from North East England.

York Minster, so well-known as a landmark to our aircrews coming and going on their missions, is a perfect choice for this memorial to the many thousands of airmen from this country and others of the Commonwealth and Empire, and from Allied countries, who went out from bases in the North and did not return [...]

J. C. Slessor
Marshal of the Royal Air Force
(Sir John C. Slessor GCB DSO MC Chief of the Air Staff)

THE AIRMEN'S MEMORIAL AT YORK MINSTER

The Airmen's Memorial was placed in the north transept in 1955. It is an astronomical clock showing the phases of the moon and the solstice, embodying the picturesque signs of the Zodiac. On the reverse of the clock is an astronomical map of the night skies showing the constellations in the Northern Hemisphere under which the airmen flew to their objectives. Under the clock there stands a lectern on which lies the Book of Remembrance containing the names of some 20,000 airmen who lost their lives while serving in the units and formations which the Memorial commemorates. One page of the Book is turned each week.

THEY WENT THROUGH THE AIR AND SPACE WITHOUT FEAR
AND THE SHINING STARS MARKED THEIR SHINING DEEDS

THE WAR DEAD OF THE
BRITISH COMMONWEALTH AND EMPIRE

The Register of the names of those who fell in the
1939–1945 War and are buried in Cemeteries
in France
London Cemetery Extension,
High Wood, Longueval
and Minor Cemeteries in Somme – II

Compiled and Published by Order of
The Imperial War Graves Commission
1958

Roye New British Cemetery Index No Fr. 554 Roye is a commune and small ancient town 25 miles (40 kilometres) south-east of Amiens at the intersection of the N.334 (Amiens–Soissons) and the N.17 (Lille–Paris) roads. There is a railway station [...] where taxis are available.

The New British Cemetery is a mile south-east of the town on the N.334 road. It dates from the 1914–1918 War, having been created after the Armistice to bury the dead from the surrounding battlefields and from other burial grounds [...]

The 1939–1945 War burials were all airmen, comprising 36 belonging to the Royal Air Force; 3 to the Royal Canadian Air Force; 2 to the Royal Australian Air Force and 2 to the Royal New Zealand Air Force, making a total of 43 [...]

Dixon, Flying Officer (Bomb Aimer) Herbert Donald, 125643. RAF (VR) 78 Sqdn. 16th April, 1943. Age 29. Son of the Revd. Herbert Henry Dixon, MA, and Jessie Maud Dixon, of Manaccan Vicarage, Cornwall. MA (Cantab) Magdalene College. Plot 1. Row AA. Grave 16.

Illingworth, Sgt. (Pilot) William, 1387760. RAF (VR) 78 Sqdn. 16th April 1943. Son of Ernest and Rose Illingworth; husband of Lilian Doris Illingworth of Forest Gate, Essex. Plot 1. Row AA. Grave 13.

Patton, Sgt. (Air Gunner) Sydney William, 1384483. RAF (VR) 78 Sqdn. 16th April 1943. Age 21. Son of Sydney Covell Patton and Alice Maud Patton, of Brixton, London. Plot 1. Row AA. Grave 12.

Thomas, Sgt. (W.Op/Air Gnr) Edwin Gordon, 1270671. RAF (VR) 78 Sqdn. 16th April 1943. Age 21. Son of Edwin Gordon Thomas and Helen Thomas, of Wanstead, Essex. Plot 1. Row AA. Grave 14.

WATKINS, Sgt. (Air Gnr.) David Aubrey, 1652776. RAF (VR) 78 Sqdn. 16th April 1943. Age 20. Son of Aubrey Wilfred and Clara Novello Watkins of Brynmill, Swansea. Plot 1. Row AA. Grave 17.

WEST, Sgt. (Nav.) Clifford George, 1316504. RAF (VR) 78 Sqdn. 16th April 1943. Son of William Albert and Clarice Winifred West of Morriston, Swansea. Plot 1. Row AA. Grave 15.

WOODHALL, Sgt. (Flt. Eng.) Ronald, 995589. RAF (VR) 78 Sqdn. 16th April 1943. Age 22. Son of Robert Woodhall and Annie E. Woodhall of Full Sutton, Yorkshire. Plot 1. Row AA. Grave 11.

THE ROYAL AIR FORCE CHURCH
OF ST CLEMENT DANES
in the Strand, London, w.c.2.

DEDICATION
OF THE ROYAL AIR FORCE
BOOKS OF REMEMBRANCE
containing the Roll of Honour
of those who died during
the Second World War

A SERVICE OF COMMEMORATION
to be conducted by
Chaplains of the Presbyterian, Methodist, Baptist
and Congregational Churches
on the weekdays
MONDAY, 8TH MAY to SATURDAY, 13TH MAY, 1961

Minister: O God, Who hast revealed Thy purpose for Mankind in Him Who is King of Righteousness and Prince of Peace, inspire the hearts of all men to follow after justice, and hasten the time when nation shall not lift up a sword against nation, neither shall they learn war anymore: through Jesus Christ our Lord.

AMEN

Edwin's mother died in 1970. She grieved her loss to the end.

INDEX